Comprehension and Language Arts Skills

Level 6

A Division of The McGraw·Hill Companies

Columbus, Ohio

www.sra4kids.com

SRA/McGraw-Hill

A Division of The McGraw-Hill Companies

Copyright © 2002 by SRA/McGraw-Hill.

Send all inquiries to:
SRA/McGraw-Hill
8787 Orion Place
Columbus, OH 43240-4027

Printed in the United States of America.

ISBN 0-07-570768-3

  4 5 6 7 8 9 POH 06 05 04 03

Table of Contents

Unit 1 **Perseverance**

Lesson 1 *The Fire Builder*
Comprehension:
Author's Purpose. 2
Grammar and Usage:
Verbs 4

Lesson 2 *Amaroq, the Wolf*
Comprehension:
Cause and Effect 6
Grammar and Usage:
Nouns. 8

Lesson 3 *On Top of the World*
Comprehension:
Sequence 10
Grammar and Usage:
Pronouns 12
Writer's Craft:
Effective Beginnings and Endings . 14

Lesson 4 *Saint George and
the Dragon*
Comprehension:
Compare and Contrast 16

Writer's Craft:
Time and Order Words. 18
Grammar and Usage:
Subjects and Predicates. 20
Writer's Craft:
Sentence Combining. 22
Writer's Craft:
Using Exact Words. 24

Lesson 5 *A Picture Book of
Jesse Owens*
Comprehension:
Drawing Conclusions 26
Mechanics:
Capitalization 28

Lesson 6 *Back to the
Drawing Board*
Comprehension:
Main Idea and Supporting Details. . 30
Grammar, Usage, and Mechanics:
Review. 32

Unit 2 **Ancient Civilizations**

Lesson 1 *Digging Up the Past*
Grammar and Usage:
Kinds of Sentences. 34
Writer's Craft:
Organizing an Expository
Paragraph 36

Lesson 2 *The Search for
Early Americans*
Comprehension:
Main Idea and Supporting Details. . 38
Grammar and Usage:
Adjectives 40
Writer's Craft:
Topic Sentences 42

Lesson 3 *The Island of Bulls*
Comprehension:
Making Inferences 44
Grammar and Usage:
Adverbs. 46
Writer's Craft:
Aim/Purpose and Audience 48

Lesson 4 *The People on the Beach*
Grammar and Usage:
Prepositions and Prepositional
Phrases 50

Writer's Craft:
Telling in Time Order 52

Lesson 5 *The Riddle of the
Rosetta Stone*
Mechanics:
Quotation Marks and
Underlining 54
Writer's Craft:
Outlining 56
Writer's Craft:
Supporting Details 58

Lesson 6 *His Majesty,
Queen Hatshepsut*
Comprehension:
Fact and Opinion 60
Grammar and Usage:
Linking Verbs, Predicate Nouns,
and Predicate Adjectives 62
Writer's Craft:
Citing Sources. 64

Lesson 7 *The Silk Route*
Grammar, Usage, and Mechanics:
Review. 66
Writer's Craft:
Passive Voice 68

Unit 3 Taking a Stand

Lesson 1 *The Pretty Pennies Picket*
Grammar and Usage:
Helping Verbs and Double Negatives 70
Writer's Craft:
Tone of a Business Letter 72

Lesson 2 *Class Discussion*
Comprehension:
Making Inferences 74
Grammar and Usage: Clauses and Subordinating Conjunctions 76
Writer's Craft:
Transition Words 78

Lesson 3 *The Grimké Sisters*
Grammar and Usage:
Participles and Participial Phrases 80

Lesson 4 *I Have a Dream*
Comprehension:
Author's Point of View 82
Grammar and Usage:
Verb Tenses 84

Lesson 5 *Gandhi*
Grammar and Usage:
Types of Sentences 86
Writer's Craft:
Sentence Variety 88

Lesson 6 *Sweeping Pittsburgh Clean*
Comprehension:
Cause and Effect 90
Grammar and Usage:
Reflexive, Intensive, and Demonstrative Pronouns 92
Writer's Craft:
Avoiding Wordiness 94

Lesson 7 *Passage to Freedom*
Grammar, Usage, and Mechanics:
Review 96

Unit 4 Beyond the Notes

Lesson 1 *What Is an Orchestra?*
Comprehension:
Classifying/Categorizing 98
Mechanics:
Parentheses and Hyphens 100
Writer's Craft:
Sentence Elaboration and Expansion 102

Lesson 2 *The Nightingale*
Grammar and Usage:
Indefinite, Relative, and Interrogative Pronouns 104
Writer's Craft:
Organization of a Narrative Paragraph` 106

Lesson 3 *Aïda*
Comprehension:
Drawing Conclusions 108
Grammar and Usage:
Appositives and Appositive Phrases 110
Writer's Craft:
Dialogue 112

Lesson 4 *The Sound of Flutes*
Mechanics:
Dashes and Colons 114
Writer's Craft: Plot 116

Writer's Craft:
Setting 118
Writer's Craft:
Characterization 120

Lesson 5 *Ray and Mr. Pit*
Comprehension:
Cause and Effect 122
Grammar and Usage:
Fragments 124
Writer's Craft:
Dialogue 126

Lesson 6 *Beethoven Lives Upstairs*
Mechanics:
Commas 128
Writer's Craft:
Effective Beginnings and Endings 130

Lesson 7 *The Man Who Wrote* Messiah
Comprehension:
Sequence 132
Grammar, Usage, and Mechanics:
Review 134
Writer's Craft:
Time and Order Words 136

Unit 5 Ecology

Lesson 1 *Protecting Wildlife*
Comprehension:
Fact and Opinion 138
Grammar and Usage:
Subject-Verb Agreement 140
Writer's Craft:
Developing Persuasive Writing . . 142

Lesson 2 *The Most Beautiful Roof in the World*
Grammar and Usage:
Direct and Indirect Objects 144
Writer's Craft:
Staying on Topic 146

Lesson 3 *Alejandro's Gift*
Comprehension:
Sequence 148
Grammar and Usage:
Perfect Tenses of Verbs 150
Writer's Craft:
Parallel Sentences 152

Lesson 4 *A Natural Force*
Grammar and Usage:
Pronouns and Antecedents 154
Writer's Craft:
Exaggeration. 156

Lesson 5 *Saving the Peregrine Falcon*
Comprehension:
Cause and Effect 158
Grammar and Usage:
Sentence Problems. 160
Writer's Craft:
Fact Versus Opinion. 162

Lesson 6 *The Day They Parachuted Cats on Borneo*
Grammar, Usage, and Mechanics:
Review. 164
Writer's Craft:
Transition Words 166

Unit 6 A Question of Value

Lesson 1 *King Midas*
Comprehension:
Author's Purpose 168
Grammar, Usage, and Mechanics:
Review. 170
Writer's Craft:
Sensory Detail 172

Lesson 2 *A Brother's Promise*
Grammar, Usage, and Mechanics:
Review. 174
Writer's Craft:
Organizing a Descriptive
Paragraph 176
Writer's Craft:
Exact Words 178

Lesson 3 *A Gift for a Gift*
Grammar, Usage, and Mechanics:
Review. 180
Writer's Craft:
Sound of Language. 182

Lesson 4 *The Gold Coin*
Comprehension:
Author's Purpose 184
Grammar, Usage, and Mechanics:
Review. 186
Writer's Craft:
Sound of Language. 188

Lesson 5 *The No-Guitar Blues*
Grammar, Usage, and Mechanics:
Review. 190
Writer's Craft:
Figurative Language. 192

Lesson 6 *The Quiltmaker's Gift*
Comprehension:
Drawing Conclusions. 194
Grammar, Usage, and Mechanics:
Review. 196
Writer's Craft:
Order of Details 198

Author's Purpose

Focus The author's purpose is his or her reason for writing a selection.

> ▶ The **author's purpose** might be to inform, to explain, to entertain, or to persuade.
> ▶ An author can have more than one purpose in writing.

Identify

Look through "The Fire Builder" and identify the author's purpose in writing the selection. Write two sentences from the story that show how the author achieved his purpose. Then, explain how you think each sentence shows the author's purpose.

Author's purpose: _____

_____

Page: _____

Sentence: _____

_____

_____

Explanation: _____

_____

_____

Page: _____

Sentence: _____

_____

_____

Explanation: _____

_____

UNIT 1 Perseverance • **Lesson 1** *The Fire Builder*

▶ Author's Purpose

COMPREHENSION

Practice

For each book title below, identify the author's purpose.

1. *How to Build a Better Birdhouse*

_____

2. *Attack of the Giant Ant Creatures from Outer Space*

_____

3. *Vacation Guide to Philadelphia*

_____

4. *Why You Should Be a Vegetarian*

_____

Apply

Choose one of the above book titles and write a paragraph that might be used on the back cover of the book to attract readers. Be sure to keep the purpose in mind.

_____

_____

_____

_____

_____

_____

_____

_____

_____

_____

_____

Verbs

A verb tells what a person, place, or thing is doing or has, or it tells about a state of being.

Rule	Example
▶ A verb can express a state of being.	▶ Sir Isaac Newton **was** a scientist. His discoveries **remain** important today.
▶ An action verb expresses a mental or physical action.	▶ Newton **wondered** why objects fall to the ground. (mental action) He **experimented** with the forces of gravity. (physical action)
▶ An action verb can also tell what a subject has.	▶ Newton **had** many ideas.
▶ When a verb is in the active voice, the subject performs the action.	▶ Newton **discovered** the law of gravity.
▶ When a verb is in the passive voice, the subject receives the action.	▶ The law of gravity **was discovered** by Newton.

Circle all of the verbs in the following paragraph.

The *G.* in Warren G. Harding, the 29th president of the United States, stands for "Gamaliel." Harding began his political career in the Ohio Senate in 1900. Then, in 1915, he became a U.S. senator. A member of the Republican party, Harding was a presidential candidate in 1920. He won the election that year with seven million more votes than his opponent. As president, Harding worked for peace between Germany and the U.S. after World War I. He died in 1923, near the end of his only term as president.

►**Verbs**

GRAMMAR AND USAGE

Practice

Circle the verb in each sentence and tell whether it expresses a mental or physical action, ownership, or a state of being.

1. Warren G. Harding and Calvin Coolidge were running mates in 1920.

   _____

2. Coolidge graduated from Amherst College in 1895. _____

3. In 1923, Coolidge became president. _____

4. He believed in reducing income taxes. _____

5. He had an interest in the Paris Pact. _____

6. Congress passed the Soldier Bonus Act despite the president's veto.

   _____

7. Historians think of Coolidge as a man of few words. _____

Proofread

In the space below, rewrite the following passage, changing the verb in each sentence from the passive to the active voice.

From an early age, Benjamin Franklin was seized by a desire to write and publish his own works. His *Autobiography* is considered by many to be a classic. *Poor Richard's Almanac,* founded in 1732, was also written by Franklin. Today, he is remembered by Americans as a man of great wisdom and practicality.

_____

_____

_____

_____

_____

_____

UNIT 1 Perseverance • **Lesson 2** *Amaroq, the Wolf*

Cause and Effect

Focus A cause-and-effect relationship helps readers understand why events happen in a certain way.

> ▸ A **cause** is an event that brings about other events. It is the reason that something happens.
> ▸ The events brought about are called **effects**. They are the things that happen.
> ▸ An **effect** can become the cause of other effects.
> ▸ Writers often use signal words and phrases to identify **cause-and-effect** relationships. These words include *because, so, if, then, since, for, as a result, therefore,* and *for this reason.*

Identify

Look through "Amaroq, the Wolf." Find one event (cause) that leads to additional events (effects). Write the cause and effects below. If the effects you have written lead to further effects, follow the arrows and write them.

Cause: _____

_____

_____

Effect: _____

_____

_____

Further Effects: _____

_____

_____

_____

▶**Cause and Effect**

Practice

Write a possible cause for each of the following effects.

1. Cause: _____

Effect: *The car's tire was flat.* _____

_____

2. Cause: _____

Effect: *Everyone laughed except for Leo.* _____

_____

3. Cause: _____

Effect: *Marta ran into the store, holding a dollar bill in her hand.* _____

4. Cause: _____

Effect: *The dog trotted down to the riverbank and barked.* _____

Apply

Continue the story of "Amaroq, the Wolf," explaining what effect Amaroq's acceptance will have on Miyax's situation.

_____

_____

_____

_____

_____

_____

_____

_____

COMPREHENSION

Nouns

A noun names a person, place, thing, or idea.

Rule	**Example**
▶ A common noun names any person, place, thing, or idea.	▶ city doctors
▶ A proper noun names a specific person, place, thing, or idea. Proper nouns are always capitalized.	▶ Dr. Lin New York City
▶ A concrete noun can be observed or touched.	▶ water brick
▶ An abstract noun cannot be observed or touched.	▶ truth beauty
▶ A compound noun contains two or more words. Compound nouns can be concrete or abstract. Also, they can be hyphenated, written as one word, or written as two words.	▶ classroom (concrete) back yard (concrete) weekend (abstract) get-together (abstract)

Circle the proper nouns in the following paragraph. Underline the common nouns.

Franklin D. Roosevelt was an inspiration to many Americans. Roosevelt became president of the United States in 1933, during the Great Depression. Most citizens were suffering, and many were starving. President Roosevelt often addressed the nation in radio talks and spoke about his hopes and ideals. He also guided the country through World War II. He met many times with Winston Churchill, the prime minister of Great Britain, and Joseph Stalin, the leader of the Soviet Union.

▶ **Nouns**

Practice

Write whether each underlined noun is abstract or concrete. Circle the two underlined compound nouns.

1. Miyax needed <u>help</u> from the black wolves. _____

2. She could see the wolves from the top of the <u>frost heave</u>.

   _____

3. The wolves made sounds and movements that expressed <u>friendship</u>.

   _____

4. Miyax's <u>father</u> had taught her the value of patience. _____

5. Miyax imitated the squirrels' signal with her <u>forefinger</u>.

   _____

6. It was clear that the black wolf possessed <u>wisdom</u>. _____

7. With <u>kindness</u> in her eyes, Miyax looked at the wolf. _____

8. Her <u>stomach</u> ached with hunger. _____

9. The food she had carried in her <u>backpack</u> was gone. _____

10. When the wolves' eyes met hers, Miyax's <u>heart</u> beat quickly.

    _____

Proofread

Put three lines under the letters of the proper nouns that should be capitalized.

   Plateaus are flat, raised areas of land. One of the most famous plateaus in the united states is the colorado plateau, which is just west of the rocky mountains. Over millions of years, the colorado river cut deeply into the rocks of the plateau and formed the grand canyon. This canyon is an enormous valley in arizona that is more than a mile deep. Most of the canyon is part of the grand canyon national park.

UNIT I   Perseverance • **Lesson 3** *On Top of the World*

Sequence

Focus Good writers arrange story events into a logical sequence so that readers can understand the order in which the events occur.

▶ **Time and order words tell** readers when events in a story take place.

▶ Some words that indicate **time** are *yesterday, tomorrow, morning, night, moment, minute, suddenly,* and *last year.*

▶ Some words that indicate **order** are *first, last, after, next, finally,* and *then.*

Identify

Look through "On Top of the World." Find examples of words or phrases used by the author to indicate a certain amount of time, a certain time of day, or the order in which events occur.

1. Page: _____

Word or phrase: _____

_____

2. Page: _____

Word or phrase: _____

_____

3. Page: _____

Word or phrase: _____

_____

4. Page: _____

Word or phrase: _____

_____

5. Page: _____

Word or phrase: _____

_____

UNIT I Perseverance • **Lesson 3** *On Top of the World*

Practice

Read each sentence. Then fill in the blanks with a word or a phrase that indicates time or order.

1. She ate breakfast, _____ she did the dishes.

2. _____ the car accident, the driver was taken to the hospital.

3. I stayed home _____, but today I went out.

4. Put on your socks _____ you put on your shoes.

Apply

Write a paragraph about things that happened in your school last week. Be sure to include time and order words to help the reader understand when each event took place.

_____

_____

_____

_____

_____

_____

_____

_____

_____

_____

_____

_____

_____

_____

_____

COMPREHENSION

UNIT I Perseverance • **Lesson 3** *On Top of the World*

Pronouns

A pronoun takes the place of a noun or nouns.

Rule	**Example**
▶ Personal pronouns refer to people or things. A personal pronoun can be the subject of a sentence.	▶ William Faulkner was a great American writer. **He** lived in Mississippi. (subject pronoun)
▶ A personal pronoun can also be the object of a verb or a preposition. An object pronoun answers the question *whom, what, for whom, to whom,* or *to what.*	▶ Mary gave **me** a copy of *Light in August.* (answers the question *to whom*) That book interests **her.** (answers the question *whom*) The author is Faulkner. Many awards were given to **him.** (object of the preposition, answers the question *to whom*)
▶ Possessive pronouns show who or what has something. They are not written with apostrophes.	▶ Eudora Welty also won many awards for **her** novels.
▶ Some possessive pronouns stand alone.	▶ In 1973, the Pulitzer Prize for Fiction was **hers.**
▶ Don't confuse the contraction *it's* with the possessive pronoun *its.*	▶ The plot of *Light in August* is its best feature. It's hard to say whose novel is better.

Underline the subject pronouns once and the object pronouns twice. Circle the possessive pronouns.

Have you read William Shakespeare's play *Romeo and Juliet?* It takes place in Verona, Italy. When Romeo meets Juliet, he immediately falls in love with her. However, her father wants her to marry Count Paris. Defying her father, Juliet pledges her love to Romeo and promises to marry him. They exchange wedding vows in secret. When Romeo is banished from the city, Juliet finds an apothecary who gives her a sleeping potion. Romeo thinks that she is dead, so he takes poison and dies. Once Juliet wakes up, she sees Romeo and stabs her chest with his dagger. Their families had been enemies, but the tragic deaths of Romeo and Juliet give them a reason to reunite.

UNIT 1 Perseverance • **Lesson 3** *On Top of the World*

► **Pronouns**

GRAMMAR AND USAGE

Practice

Circle the correct pronoun or pronouns.

1. My friend Evan and (me/I) love the music of Louis Armstrong.

2. Evan's great-uncle gave (him and me/he and I) a recording of "What a Wonderful World" by Armstrong.

3. Armstrong knew many musicians; (he/him) and "King" Oliver's Creole Jazz Band played in Chicago during the 1920s.

4. A singing style called scat was invented by (him/he).

5. Scat sounds choppy because (its/it's) rhythm is based on syllables instead of words.

6. Armstrong married many times; Daisy Parker was (him's/his) first wife.

7. In 1925, Armstrong's new band gave (him/he) a chance to be the leader.

8. When Armstrong went to Denmark in 1933, ten thousand people greeted (he/him) at the train station.

9. Louis Armstrong's music is still (ours/our's) to enjoy.

10. Armstrong is (my/mine) favorite musician.

Proofread

Write the correct pronoun above each underlined word or words.

Many of the characters in *Alice in Wonderland* are animals. Some of the <u>animals</u> attend a tea party. <u>The tea party</u> seems very humorous to Alice, but <u>Alice</u> is confused. Nothing makes sense to <u>Alice</u>. The March Hare and the Mad Hatter speak in riddles, and Alice doesn't understand the meaning of the <u>March Hare's and the Mad Hatter's</u> words. Later, Alice is amazed when the Cheshire Cat disappears; nothing is left but <u>the Cheshire Cat's</u> smile.

UNIT 1 Perseverance • **Lesson 3** *On Top of the World*

Effective Beginnings and Endings

An effective beginning captures the reader's attention. An effective ending gives the reader a sense of completeness and leaves the reader with something to reflect on.

Rule

▶ To write a good beginning:
  - Begin with a quotation or with dialogue.
  - Ask a question or tell an interesting fact, or both.
  - Invite the reader into the scene using sensory details, telling an anecdote, or both.
▶ To write a good ending:
  - Sum up your main points.
  - Answer any questions that have not yet been answered.
  - Introduce a new idea to keep the reader thinking about your writing.

Example

▶ "Would you rather travel by plane or by hot-air balloon?" my friend asked.
▶ Did you know that a hot-air balloon can travel up to 70 miles per hour?
▶ Picture a small child being dazzled by gigantic, rainbow-colored balloons in the sky. That was me in 1995.
▶ So, the next time you fly on an airplane, imagine that you are traveling on a giant bird.

 **Try It!** **Write an effective beginning and ending for the following type of writing.**

1. Article about your favorite place to visit

_____

_____

_____

_____

_____

_____

_____

_____

_____

UNIT I Perseverance • **Lesson 3** *On Top of the World*

Effective Beginnings and Endings

Practice

Tell if you think each beginning and ending is effective. Explain your answer.

Beginnings

1. Franklin Roosevelt once said that "the only thing we have to fear is fear itself." I found out just what this meant the day that I took my first flying lesson.

   _____

   _____

2. Betty loved ice skating. She dreamed of winning an Olympic gold medal. But there would be no more ice skating after next week. Her dad got laid off, and her parents just couldn't afford the lessons anymore. Betty was not ready to give up her dream, though.

   _____

   _____

3. Ants are interesting. They are very hardworking, and there are many different kinds.

   _____

   _____

Endings

4. So, the next time you throw away that aluminum can or plastic jug, remember that you are really throwing away a part of the earth.

   _____

   _____

5. That's the end of the story.

   _____

   _____

6. Will I ever try to help out a needy person again? You better believe it!

   _____

   _____

WRITER'S CRAFT

UNIT 1 Perseverance • **Lesson 4** *Saint George and the Dragon*

Compare and Contrast

Focus Good writers compare and contrast to paint a clear picture for their readers.

> ▶ To **compare** means to explain how two or more things are alike. Words used to compare include *both*, *same*, *like*, and *as*.
> ▶ To **contrast** means to explain how two or more things are different. Words used to contrast include *different*, *but*, *unlike*, and *although*.

Identify

Look at the description of the dragon on pages 66–69 of "Saint George and the Dragon." Find three examples of comparison. Write the examples on the lines below.

1. _____

_____

_____

2. _____

_____

_____

3. _____

_____

_____

UNIT 1 Perseverance • **Lesson 4** *Saint George and the Dragon*

▶ **Compare and Contrast**

Practice

Read the paragraph below. Tell how the two kinds of dogs are compared and how they are contrasted.

What does an Australian shepherd dog look like? Its general appearance—the shape of the head and body and the thickness of the coat—resembles that of a Border collie. However, Australian shepherds are much bigger than Border collies, and unlike Border collies, Australian shepherds are born without tails.

Comparison: _____

_____

_____

Contrast: _____

_____

_____

Apply

Write a paragraph that compares and contrasts two games that you know how to play.

_____

_____

_____

_____

_____

_____

_____

_____

_____

COMPREHENSION

Time and Order Words

By using time and order words, good writers arrange events in a story or other kinds of writing into a logical sequence.

▶ Time and order words help readers understand the order in which the events occur.

▶ Some words that indicate **time** include *yesterday, tomorrow, morning, night, afternoon, moment, minute, hour, suddenly, now, immediately, last year,* and *last week.*

▶ Some words that indicate **order** are *first, second, last, after, next, finally,* and *then.*

 **Try It!** **For each example, identify the time and order words used to make the sequence of events clearer.**

1. As soon as he woke up in the morning, the little boy jumped out of bed and ran to the window. Snow! He hastily put on his coat and hat and then pulled on his boots and gloves. He darted outside. A few paces from his doorstep, he paused for a few moments, taking in the sparkling white blanket of fresh snow that covered the ground. Next, he flopped on his back and then moved his arms and legs back and forth in the snow. Finally, he stood up and turned around to look at his very first snow angel of the year.

_____

2. To fill up the gas tank in your car, the first thing you need to do is to turn the car off. Next, get out of the car and open the gas tank. Once you have the lid off the gas tank, remove the gas nozzle from the gas pump, and then push up the lever it was resting on. Insert the nozzle into the gas tank. After the zeroes stop blinking on the screen of the gas pump, squeeze the handle of the gas nozzle. Depending on how much gas you need, it will take anywhere from a few seconds to a minute or so to fill up the tank. When the tank is full, put lid back on. Finally, pay the cashier.

_____

UNIT I Perseverance • **Lesson 4** *Saint George and the Dragon*

▶ **Time and Order Words**

Practice

Read each sentence. Then fill in the blanks with a word or a phrase that indicates time or order.

1. She ate breakfast, _____ she did the dishes.

2. Just _____ the accident, the driver dialed her cell phone.

3. I stayed home _____, but today I went out.

4. _____ a squirrel darted across the road, and the car swerved.

5. I will start reading *Baseball in April and Other Stories*

   _____.

6. For the first few _____ of his workout, he did some stretching exercises.

7. _____ in the morning is the worst time to leave for school.

Choose the time or order word from the box that best completes the sentence.

yesterday	tomorrow	night	minute
now	first	then	suddenly

1. _____ I was late for school.

2. I'll have to stay up late to study for my math test _____.

3. It takes only a _____ to heat up a burrito in the microwave.

4. The girls spent the _____ at a sleepover.

5. "Tricia, come here _____!" my mom yelled.

6. _____ stir in the spices, and _____ add the potatoes.

7. The thunder roared, and the lights went out _____.

WRITER'S CRAFT

Subjects and Predicates

Every sentence has a subject and a predicate. The subject tells whom or what the sentence is about, and the predicate tells what the subject does, has, is, or is like.

Rule

- The simple subject is the main subject without its modifiers.
- The simple predicate is the main verb or verbs.
- The complete subject includes the main subject and all of its modifiers.
- The complete predicate includes all of the words in the predicate of a sentence.
- A compound subject is two or more simple subjects that have the same predicate.
- When two or more simple subjects are joined by *or, either . . . or,* or *neither . . . nor,* the verb agrees with the nearest subject.
- A compound predicate is two or more simple predicates that have the same subject.

Example

- All **animals** are multicellular organisms.
- All animals **are** multicellular organisms.
- **All animals** are multicellular organisms.
- All animals **are multicellular organisms.**
- **Insects, spiders,** and **shrimp** are arthropods.
- **Neither** an octopus **nor** a snail **is** an arthropod.
  Neither an oyster **nor** any kinds of lobsters **are** reptiles.
- Many sponges **have** no shape and **live** attached to one place.

 **Try It!** **Underline each complete subject once and each complete predicate twice.**

1. Oklahoma, Arkansas, and Louisiana border the state of Texas.

2. The southern border of Texas is formed by the Rio Grande.

3. Oil fields in Texas produce millions of gallons of petroleum.

4. Petroleum is refined and used in the production of gasoline, kerosene, and paints.

5. Dallas, Houston, and San Antonio are the largest cities in Texas.

UNIT I Perseverance • **Lesson 4** *Saint George and the Dragon*

▶ Subjects and Predicates

Practice

Draw a vertical line between the complete subject and the complete predicate in each sentence. Underline each simple subject once and each simple predicate twice. Remember that simple subjects and predicates can be compound.

6. The solar system has the sun at its center and includes nine planets.

7. Mercury, Venus, Mars, and Earth are the inner planets.

8. All of the planets have similar compositions.

9. Jupiter, Saturn, Uranus, Neptune, and Pluto comprise the outer planets.

10. Except for Pluto, the outer planets are composed of hot gases and have several moons.

11. In addition, the solar system includes asteroids, meteors, and comets.

12. Streaking through the sky, comets leave behind trails of hot gases.

13. Meteors streak through the sky as well.

14. Another name for a meteor is a shooting star.

15. Occasionally, meteorites survive the plunge to Earth and reach its surface.

Proofread

Circle the verb that agrees with the subject of each sentence.

Charlotte, Emily, and Anne Brontë (was/were) all writers. Neither Emily nor Anne (was/were) as well known as Charlotte. Either *Wuthering Heights* or *Jane Eyre* (is/are) the most popular of the Brontë sisters' novels. Neither Charlotte nor her sisters (was/were) very outgoing. Charlotte and her sisters still (has/have) many loyal readers.

GRAMMAR AND USAGE

UNIT I   Perseverance • **Lesson 4** *Saint George and the Dragon*

Sentence Combining

To add style and variety to your writing, you can combine sentences.

Rule	**Example**
▶ Create a compound sentence by combining two short, simple sentences that are closely related. To do this, use a comma and a conjunction such as *and*, *but*, or *or*.	▶ Eric wanted to play football. His parents wouldn't let him. Eric wanted to play football, but his parents wouldn't let him.
▶ Create compound subjects and verbs.	▶ Liza liked eggplant. Geraldo liked eggplant. Liza and Geraldo liked eggplant. (compound subject)
▶ Combine ideas from two or more shorter sentences by using phrases, such as appositives and prepositional phrases.	▶ Thomas Edison was an American scientist and inventor. He had more than 1,000 patents. Thomas Edison, **an American scientist and inventor**, had more than 1,000 patents. (appositive) Edison moved from Menlo Park. He moved to West Orange, New Jersey. Edison moved from Menlo Park **to West Orange, New Jersey.** (prepositional phrase)

 **Try It!**   **For each sentence, tell if it is a compound sentence or if it includes a compound subject or verb, a prepositional phrase, or an appositive.**

1. Edison invented and tested the movie camera. _____

2. Edison announced and demonstrated his most important invention,

   the incandescent light bulb. _____

3. The light bulb was a great success, and Edison immediately sought to

   improve it. _____

4. Nikola Tesla and George Westinghouse developed the

   alternating-current method. _____

5. Edison announced his invention of a phonograph. _____

UNIT I Perseverance • **Lesson 4** *Saint George and the Dragon*

Sentence Combining

Practice

Combine the sentences in each numbered exercise to create one longer sentence.

1. a. In 1862 Edison published a weekly newspaper.

   b. The newspaper was called the *Grand Trunk Herald*.

   _____

   _____

2. a. Edison received the Albert Medal of the Society of Arts of Great Britain.

   b. Edison also received the Congressional Gold Medal.

   _____

   _____

3. a. The Kinetoscope was one type of projector invented by Edison.

   b. The Vitascope was another type of projector invented by Edison.

   _____

   _____

4. a. In his later life, Edison improved his inventions.

   b. At the same time, Edison perfected his inventions.

   _____

   _____

5. a. Thomas Edison was an American inventor.

   b. He helped shape modern society with his inventions.

   _____

   _____

WRITER'S CRAFT

UNIT 1 Perseverance • **Lesson 4** *Saint George and the Dragon*

Using Exact Words

To make your writing sharp and clear, use exact words. Words that say exactly what you mean to say make your writing easier to understand and more enjoyable to read.

The following tips can help you choose the most exact words when writing:

▶ Be specific. For example, instead of saying something is *blue*, use a more exact word such as *turquoise*. This tells what *kind* of blue it is.

▶ Decide what feeling you want to give the reader through your words. The feeling connected with a word is called its *connotation*. For example, saying *I strode into class* instead of *I walked into class* suggests that you felt confident when you entered the room. The more exact word *strode* tells *how* you walked. Some words have a positive connotation, such as *strode*. Others have a negative connotation, such as *strutted*, which suggests a false sense of pride.

▶ Avoid words that are used over and over again. Words such as *good* and *interesting* are used so much that they don't have much meaning.

 **Try It!** **For each sentence, tell which word in parentheses is more exact, and why.**

1. The student (slouched, sat) in the chair.

_____

2. The baby (cried, wailed) when she was hungry.

_____

3. The audience (laughed, cackled) at the comedian's joke.

_____

4. The cat's (inky, dark) fur shone in the light.

_____

UNIT I Perseverance • **Lesson 4** *Saint George and the Dragon*

▶ **Using Exact Words**

Practice

Read each pair of words. Then circle the word with the more positive connotation. Briefly explain your choice.

1. mob, gathering: _____

2. piglet, runt: _____

3. courageous, foolhardy: _____

4. statesman, politician: _____

5. penny-pinching, thrifty: _____

6. athlete, jock: _____

Rewrite each sentence by changing the underlined words to more exact words. The new words should have the same general meaning but should be more specific; they may also have a more obvious connotation.

1. The light-colored dog walked in the park.

   _____

2. The car going down the street was green.

   _____

3. Did you see the bright star moving through the sky last night?

   _____

4. A brown leaf fell from the tree.

   _____

5. The house was big and dark.

   _____

WRITER'S CRAFT

Drawing Conclusions

Focus Readers draw conclusions about the characters and events in a story by using information the writer provides in the text with information they already know.

> ▶ Readers use the information in the text and what they already know to draw conclusions about characters or events in a story.
> ▶ Readers' conclusions should be supported with information in the text.

Practice

On the following lines, write information the writer provides about Jesse Owens in "A Picture Book of Jesse Owens."

_____

_____

_____

_____

_____

Then, use the above information to draw conclusions about Jesse Owens and his accomplishments.

_____

_____

_____

_____

_____

_____

UNIT I Perseverance • **Lesson 5** *A Picture Book of Jesse Owens*

Drawing Conclusions

Read the following sentences. Then use this information to draw a conclusion.

- Zach plays basketball with his friends three times a week.

- Zach's favorite basketball team is the Lakers.

- Kobe Bryant is his favorite basketball player.

Conclusion: _____

_____

_____

_____

_____

COMPREHENSION

Capitalization

Take a look at the following rules of capitalization.

Rule	**Example**
▶ Capitalize the first word of a sentence.	▶ The sun is a star.
▶ Capitalize the names of people and their initials.	▶ B. J. Thomas
▶ Capitalize a title when it comes before a person's name or when it substitutes for a person's name.	▶ President Abraham Lincoln Are you ready, Doctor?
▶ Do not capitalize a title that follows a person's name.	▶ Abraham Lincoln was our sixteenth president.
▶ Capitalize the names of states, cities, countries, and continents.	▶ Maine, Madrid, Spain, Europe
▶ Capitalize the names of specific sections of a country. Do not capitalize other compass-direction words.	▶ the South southern New Mexico
▶ Capitalize the names of specific geographical features.	▶ Lake Tahoe
▶ Capitalize days, months, and holidays.	▶ one Friday in July Thanksgiving Day

Try It! Write the following items using proper capitalization.

1. dr. tamara jackson _____

2. president ulysses s. grant _____

3. george washington, our first president _____

4. the shore of the gulf of mexico _____

5. new orleans, louisiana _____

6. the tip of south america _____

7. the republic of china _____

8. the fourth of july, independence day _____

UNIT I Perseverance • **Lesson 5** *A Picture Book of Jesse Owens*

Practice

Circle the words that should be capitalized.

The united states bought 827,987 square miles of land from france on april 30, 1803. at that time, napoleon bonaparte was the emperor of france, and thomas jefferson was our president. the land, called the louisiana territory, extended from canada to mexico. some of the states that were part of this territory included arkansas, kansas, nebraska, and oklahoma. the land was bordered by the mississippi river in the east and by the rocky mountains in the west. the purchase of this territory doubled the size of the united states of america.

Proofread

Put three lines under each letter that should be capitalized.

Although france no longer controlled the mississipi valley after the united states purchased the louisiana territory, spain still owned parts of florida and texas. general andrew jackson had defeated the troops of great britain in new orleans in 1815. thus, the americans gained access to the west. leaving from st. louis, missouri, lewis and clark explored this region. they reached the pacific ocean by traveling down the columbia river.

MECHANICS

Main Idea and Supporting Details

Focus   Good writers organize their writing in ways that make it clearer and easier to understand.

> Writers organize their writing by using main ideas and supporting details. The **main idea** is what a paragraph or passage is mostly about. The **supporting details** provide more information about the main idea.
> ▶ A main idea may be stated in a topic sentence.
> ▶ Sometimes the main idea is not directly stated but is expressed through the supporting details.

Identify

Look through "Back to the Drawing Board" and choose one paragraph. Answer the following questions about the paragraph.

Page: _____   Paragraph: _____

What is the main idea of the paragraph?

_____

_____

_____

Is the main idea stated in a topic sentence or implied in the supporting details? Write the topic sentence of the paragraph, if there is one.

_____

_____

_____

How are the sentences of the paragraph related?

_____

_____

_____

UNIT 1 Perseverance • **Lesson 6** *Back to the Drawing Board*

▶ **Main Idea and Supporting Details**

Practice

Read each main idea. Then write three detail sentences that support this idea.

Main idea: Friends are people who try to help you.

Supporting details: _____

_____

_____

_____

Main idea: Art can be made from many different materials.

Supporting details: _____

_____

_____

_____

Main idea: Machines are part of our everyday life.

Supporting details: _____

_____

_____

_____

Main idea: Writing things helps you remember them.

Supporting details: _____

_____

_____

_____

COMPREHENSION

UNIT 1 Perseverance • **Lesson 6** *Back to the Drawing Board/Crazy Boys*

Review

Nouns and Verbs

Circle each proper noun and underline each common noun. Write whether the verb is an action or a state-of-being verb.

1. John D. Rockefeller, Jr., was a philanthropist.

_____

2. In 1901, he founded Rockefeller University in New York City.

_____

3. In addition, he had an interest in the Museum of Modern Art.

_____

4. One of his projects involved the restoration of colonial

Williamsburg, Virginia. _____

5. Today, people remember Rockefeller as an important member of

American society. _____

Possessive Nouns and Pronouns

Put three lines under each letter that should be capitalized.

the word *circus* and the name *p.t. barnum* will be forever linked in u.s. history. phineas taylor barnum was born on july 5, 1810, in bethel, connecticut. when he was twenty-four years old, barnum moved to new york city to work as a shopkeeper. his interest in entertainment led him to buy john scudder's american museum in 1841. many people came to see the museum's wax figures and other unusual attractions. president lincoln and england's queen victoria were among the famous people who were interested in barnum's exhibits. in 1881, barnum achieved his greatest fame when he and james a. bailey formed barnum and bailey's circus. since then, their circus has delighted audiences throughout america.

Comprehension and Language Arts Skills

UNIT I) Perseverance • **Lesson 6** *Back to the Drawing Board/Crazy Boys*

▶ **Review**

▶ Pronouns

Circle the correct pronouns.

6. "(Us/We), the People of the United States" are the first words of the U.S. Constitution.

7. According to the Constitution, the right to life, liberty, and the pursuit of happiness is (our's/ours).

8. (Its/It's) first ten amendments are called the Bill of Rights.

9. Thomas Jefferson signed the Declaration of Independence, which was drafted by (him/he).

10. (He/Him), George Washington, and John Adams all became presidents.

▶ Subject and Predicate

Draw a vertical line between the subject and predicate in each sentence. Underline the simple subject once and the simple predicate twice.

11. About 4000 different minerals exist on Earth.

12. All minerals form as a result of natural processes.

13. Magnetite and lodestone are minerals and have magnetic properties.

14. Diamonds, emeralds, and rubies form crystal shapes.

15. These minerals shine and sparkle.

16. Gold and silver are also minerals.

17. Artisans hammer and shape these minerals into fine pieces of jewelry.

18. South Africa, India, and California contained large gold deposits in the 1800s.

19. During the Gold Rush, miners discovered and mined much of the gold in California.

20. Large deposits of silver exist in Norway, Nevada, and Australia.

GRAMMAR, USAGE, AND MECHANCIS

Kinds of Sentences

There are four basic kinds of sentences. The end punctuation mark is determined by the purpose of the sentence.

Rule	**Example**
▶ A **declarative sentence** makes a statement. It ends with a period.	▶ Many Americans enjoy baseball.
▶ An **interrogative sentence** asks a question. It ends with a question mark.	▶ Did you know that baseball was invented in the 1800s?
▶ An **exclamatory sentence** expresses strong emotion. It ends with an exclamation point.	▶ What a great game that was!
▶ An **imperative sentence** gives a command or makes a request. It ends with a period. Often, the subject of an imperative sentence is an understood *you*.	▶ Check the batting order. (You) check the batting order.

Try It! **Identify each sentence as declarative, interrogative, exclamatory, or imperative.**

1. Roberto Clemente was a great baseball player. _____

2. Wasn't he born in Puerto Rico? _____

3. Clemente's major-league career began with the Brooklyn Dodgers.

   _____

4. Find out more about Roberto Clemente's baseball career. _____

5. Didn't he die in a plane crash? _____

6. What a terrible tragedy that was! _____

7. Read more about Roberto Clemente when you get a chance.

   _____

Comprehension and Language Arts Skills

Name _____ Date _____

▶ **Kinds of Sentences**

Practice

Add the correct end punctuation mark to each sentence and circle the subject. If the subject is understood, write *you* after the punctuation mark.

8. Have you ever visited the White House _____

9. It is the official residence of the U.S. president _____

10. Wasn't the White House completed in 1800 _____

11. How impressive the building is _____

12. John Adams was the first president to live there _____

13. Name the first ladies who have redecorated the White House _____

14. Which first lady hosted the first televised tour of the building _____

15. The president's assistants work in the West Wing _____

16. I would love to work at the White House _____

17. Go see it if you ever travel to our nation's capital city _____

Proofread

Correct the end punctuation in each sentence. Cross out the incorrect punctuation mark and write the correct one on the line. If the punctuation mark is correct, write *no correction*.

Are you familiar with any books by Mark Twain. _____ He

was so funny? _____ One of his stories is about a jumping frog.

_____ You should read that story? _____ I've never

laughed so loud! _____ Would you like to borrow my copy.

_____ Do you know Mark Twain's real name? _____

Wasn't it Samuel Langhorne Clemens! _____ Please find out if

that is correct! _____

GRAMMAR AND USAGE

UNIT 2 Ancient Civilizations • **Lesson I** *Digging Up the Past*

Organizing an Expository Paragraph

Because expository writing is informative, the ideas in an expository paragraph should be clearly organized. Your reader should be able to easily understand the information you are presenting.

Rule

▶ A **topic sentence** presents the main ideas of your paragraph. It usually comes first, but it can come last, summing up the information you have presented.

▶ **Supporting sentences** should follow some kind of order, such as order of importance or chronological order. In a description, you might follow the location of things, top to bottom or left to right. In a persuasive essay, you might follow a logical order, such as cause and effect.

▶ Your **closing sentence** should "wrap up" the paragraph well. It may summarize the paragraph, express an opinion, or conclude the steps you have presented in a chronological or logical order. Often it leads the reader to the next paragraph.

Example

▶ William B. Hoy should be in the Baseball Hall of Fame. He was the first outfielder ever to throw three runners out at home plate in the same game. He had 2,054 hits and 597 stolen bases in his fourteen years in the major leagues. He also batted .288. He was hearing impaired, and many people think the umpire's hand signals were invented to help him. As a great ballplayer and a historical figure, he deserves to be recognized.

Try It! **Read the paragraphs below and identify the order used for the supporting sentences: order of importance, chronological order, order of location, or logical order.**

It doesn't make sense to complain when it's raining. Rain makes plants grow, and plants help feed and clothe people. Therefore, people need rain. Remember that the next time you get mad that it's raining.

Order of supporting sentences: _____

The view from the cabin window was beautiful. The wild flowers in the yard below were blooming. The trees around the yard were beginning to bud. The mountains in the distance were still capped with snow. I could have sat there all day.

Order of supporting sentences: _____

UNIT 2 Ancient Civilizations • **Lesson I** *Digging Up the Past*

Organizing an Expository Paragraph

Practice

**Read each of the sentences below. Write whether you think it is
a topic sentence, a supporting sentence, or a closing sentence.
Then organize the sentences and write them in the form of a
well-organized expository paragraph.**

1. Then he developed a vaccine.

_____

2. In 1955, it was approved by the U.S. Public Health Service.

_____

3. Dr. Jonas Salk was responsible for wiping out polio in this country.

_____

4. It took him many years to identify the polio virus.

_____

5. A grateful country gave Salk the Congressional Medal for
Distinguished Achievement.

_____

6. The vaccine was tested on about a million schoolchildren.

_____

_____

_____

_____

_____

_____

_____

_____

_____

WRITER'S CRAFT

Name _____ Date _____

Main Idea and Supporting Details

Focus Good writers organize their writing in ways that make it clearer and easier to understand.

> The **main idea** is what a paragraph or passage is mainly about.
> The **supporting details** provide more information about the main idea.
> ▶ A **main idea** may be stated in a topic sentence.
> ▶ Sometimes the main idea is not directly stated but is expressed through the **supporting details** that give information about the main idea.

Identify

Look through "The Search for Early Americans" for examples of paragraphs that have a main idea and supporting details. Choose two examples and write the topic sentences and supporting details.

1. Page: _____

   Topic sentence: _____

   _____

   Supporting detail: _____

   _____

   Supporting detail: _____

   _____

2. Page: _____

   Topic sentence: _____

   _____

   Supporting detail: _____

   _____

   Supporting detail: _____

   _____

UNIT 2 Ancient Civilizations • **Lesson 2** *The Search for Early Americans*

Main Idea and Supporting Details

Practice

Read each main idea. Then, write three details that would support this idea.

1. Main idea: It is important to have fun.

   Detail: _____

   Detail: _____

   Detail: _____

2. Main idea: It is fascinating to watch fish in a tank.

   Detail: _____

   Detail: _____

   Detail: _____

3. Main idea: I love going to the beach.

   Detail: _____

   Detail: _____

   Detail: _____

Apply

Write a paragraph based on one of the main ideas above, using the supporting details you wrote.

_____

_____

_____

_____

_____

_____

_____

_____

COMPREHENSION

Adjectives

An adjective modifies, or describes, a noun or pronoun. Adjectives have both comparative and superlative forms.

Rule	**Example**
▶ An adjective can come before or after the noun or pronoun it modifies.	▶ The **quiet** pond is covered with algae. The pond that is covered with algae is **quiet.**
▶ When a **compound adjective** comes before the word it modifies, the adjective is hyphenated. If it comes after the word it modifies, it is not hyphenated.	▶ A **long-legged** crane is wading in the pond. The crane wading in the pond is **long legged.**
▶ The **comparative form** of an adjective compares two nouns or pronouns.	▶ Fir trees are **taller** than pear trees.
▶ The **superlative form** of an adjective compares more than two nouns or pronouns.	▶ Sequoias are the **tallest** of all trees.
▶ For most long adjectives, form the comparative by adding *more* before the adjective, and form the superlative by adding *most.*	▶ Silver is **more valuable** than iron. Gold is the **most valuable** metal.

Circle the adjectives in each sentence. Underline comparative forms once and superlative forms twice.

1. Lemurs are primitive primates.

2. These gentle, social creatures live in trees or large bushes.

3. Their habitats are the lush rain forests and the dry, rocky deserts of Madagascar.

4. Only the smaller species of lemurs are active at night.

5. The indri are some of the largest lemurs.

6. The most terrestrial species is the ring-tailed lemur, which spends half of its day on the ground.

7. Lemurs eat fruits and insects, but some are more carnivorous than others.

GRAMMAR AND USAGE

Practice

Underline the adjectives in each sentence. Draw an arrow from each adjective to the word it modifies.

8. Georgia O'Keeffe was a gifted artist.

9. Her unique style combined realistic scenery with abstract designs.

10. O'Keeffe painted the bright flowers and bleached bones of the southwestern deserts.

11. She was attracted to the deserts' never-ending landscapes.

12. Today, Georgia O'Keeffe's well-known and much-loved paintings hang in numerous galleries.

Proofread

Cross out each adjective that is used incorrectly and write the correct form above it.

Michelangelo was one of the most great artists that ever lived. He was

also the famousest sculptor in Italy during the fifteenth and sixteenth

centuries. His sculptures, such as *David* and the *Pieta*, are more large

than life. Art historians have noted that his most early sculptures are as

perfectly formed as his more late ones. The Medici Chapel contains his

completest sculptural project—a set of tombs designed to honor two

young dukes. Despite Michelangelo's great accomplishments as a

sculptor, his painting on the ceiling of the Sistine Chapel in Rome is

probably famouser than all of his sculptures. For centuries, it has

remained one of the belovedest works of art in the world.

Topic Sentences

A **topic sentence** clearly presents the main idea of a paragraph. Many topic sentences begin paragraphs, but some end paragraphs. Varying the position of your topic sentences can add variety to your writing.

Rule

▶ A strong topic sentence names a particular subject and states a direction or focus for the paragraph about that subject.

Example

▶ Although Susie Baker King Taylor was born into slavery, she became a teacher and Civil War nurse. At the age of fifteen, she cared for wounded and ill soldiers while guns boomed around her. She even worked for a time with legendary nurse Clara Barton. <u>She truly was a remarkable young woman.</u>

Read each paragraph below and underline the topic sentence.

1. Because human beings are exploring and exploiting more and more areas, the world is losing plant and animal species. Today, more than 34,000 plant species and 5,200 animal species are about to become extinct. Thousands more are lost each year before biologists can even identify them. These species are destroyed when their environments are ruined. Sometimes they are hunted to extinction. Damage can also be caused when new animals and plants are brought into an area. Pollution is a danger, as well. All of these dangers are introduced by people.

2. Planets that are outside our solar system are hard to see. They are much fainter than stars. However, astronomers can measure "wobbles" in a star's motion. The wobbles are caused by the slight gravitational pull of a planet. They show that a planet exists. It's amazing that we can discover planets we cannot see.

UNIT 2 Ancient Civilizations • **Lesson 2** *The Search for Early Americans*

►Topic Sentences

Practice

Read each group of sentences below. Then write a topic sentence to complete the paragraph.

3. Some people like to listen to classical music. Some people like hip hop. There are country music fans and rock and roll fans. I can appreciate anything but easy listening.

_____

_____

_____

4. The sky was dull and grey. The air was chilly and damp. People walked down the street with their heads bent and their eyes on the ground.

_____

_____

_____

5. There are many attractive, inexpensive frames. You can also find a pre-cut matte to provide a nice border for your picture. Putting frame, matte, and picture together requires care, but it is not difficult.

_____

_____

_____

WRITER'S CRAFT

UNIT 2 Ancient Civilizations • **Lesson 3** *The Island of Bulls*

Making Inferences

Focus Writers do not always include all the details in a story. Rather, they include pieces of information and invite readers to make inferences about a character or event.

> ▶ An inference is based on information from the text and on personal experience and knowledge. Inferences can be based on such information from the text as examples, facts, reasons, and descriptions. Inferences based on personal experience or knowledge should be supported by information in the selection.

Identify

Look through "The Island of Bulls" and make two inferences about an event or a character in the story. List the information from the story used to make each inference.

1. Page: _____

Inference: _____

_____

Information: _____

_____

_____

_____

2. Page: _____

Inference: _____

_____

Information: _____

_____

_____

UNIT 2 Ancient Civilizations • **Lesson 3** *The Island of Bulls*

▶**Making Inferences**

Practice

Read each pair of sentences. Then make an inference from the
information.

1. King Minos was powerful and greatly feared and was able to demand
and get whatever he wished. The king of Athens sent King Minos
14 youths to lead into the labyrinth.

   Inference: _____

   _____

   _____

   _____

2. As Theseus went into the maze he unwound the ball of thread. He
then picked up the thread and followed it out of the labyrinth.

   Inference: _____

   _____

   _____

   _____

3. Crete has a long history. In 455 B.C., Thucydides wrote an account of
King Minos. Aristotle later wrote of King Minos. Plato mentioned the
kingdom of Atlantis, which could be a reference to Crete, in his
writing around 400 B.C.

   Inference: _____

   _____

   _____

   _____

COMPREHENSION

Name _____ Date _____

UNIT 2 Ancient Civilizations • **Lesson 3** *The Island of Bulls*

Adverbs

An adverb modifies a verb, an adjective, or another adverb. Adverbs have both comparative and superlative forms.

Rule	**Example**
▶ Many adverbs are formed by adding *-ly* to an adjective. Others do not end in *-ly*.	▶ It takes **almost** 24 hours for Earth to rotate **completely** around the sun.
▶ When an adverb modifies an adjective or another adverb, it usually comes before the word	▶ The sun is made of **very** hot gases. These gases **quite** often trigger nuclear fusion reactions.
▶ When an adverb modifies a verb, the adverb can be in different positions in the sentence.	▶ Meteors **frequently** strike the moon. **Frequently,** meteors strike the moon. Meteors strike the moon **frequently.**
▶ The **comparative form** of an adverb compares two actions. For most short adverbs, add *-er* to form the comparative.	▶ Mercury orbits **nearer** to the sun than any other planet does.
▶ The **superlative form** of an adverb compares more than two actions. For most short adverbs, add *-est* to form the superlative.	▶ Of all the planets orbiting the sun, Mercury travels **fastest.**
▶ For most long adverbs and some short adverbs, form the comparative by adding *more* before the adverb, and form the superlative by adding *most*.	▶ Earth is **more volcanically** active than the moon. Jupiter's largest moon is the **most volcanically** active object in the solar system.

 **Circle the adverbs in each sentence. Draw an arrow from each adverb to the word it modifies.**

Eagles can see clearly from very great distances. Their vision is more highly developed than the vision of most other animals. Eagles often soar upward to great heights. Then, they swoop down to quickly capture their prey. Eagles most often prey on mice, snakes, and small birds.

46 UNIT 2 • Lesson 3   Comprehension and Language Arts Skills

▶**Adverbs**

GRAMMAR AND USAGE

Practice

Write the comparative and superlative forms of each adverb.

1. quietly _____ _____

2. early _____ _____

3. gently _____ _____

4. hard _____ _____

5. late _____ _____

6. low _____ _____

7. loudly _____ _____

8. deeply _____ _____

9. high _____ _____

10. fancifully _____ _____

Proofread

Cross out each adverb that is used incorrectly and write the correct form above it.

Soccer is the sport played oftenest throughout the world. However, it has gained popularity slower in the United States than in other countries. This has been changing quick. In recent years, Americans have competed successfullier in worldwide tournaments than many people ever expected. At the 1994 World Cup competition, the U.S. team often played more hard and ran more best than the other teams in its region. Brazil still won in the final game against Italy, which was the closest of the tournament. However, Americans proved that they are a team to watch close in the coming years.

Aim/Purpose and Audience

Aim/purpose and audience determine how you plan and organize your writing.

Rule	**Example**
▶ **Aim** is your specific reason for writing. **Purpose** is the general goal you wish to accomplish. Common purposes for writing are to explain, to inform, to entertain, and to persuade.	▶ The aim of your essay is to warn people about the danger of possible bear attacks in national parks. Your purpose is to inform park-goers.
▶ **Audience** refers to your readers. Your writing should appeal to their interests, experience, and level of understanding.	▶ If you're writing to inform a group of second-graders about American grizzly bears, you would use simple language to communicate basic information.

Try It! **Read the paragraphs below and write what you think the author's general purpose is for each one.**

1. I have only one thing to say about voting: do it! People who don't vote are refusing to do their duty as citizens. They have no right to complain about elected officials they didn't help to choose. So vote if you want your voice to be heard.

   _____

2. The centipede is not an insect. In fact, it can be useful for killing insects. It is a *myriapod*, which means "many legs." The centipede is covered with a hard shell that is made of different pieces, or segments. Each segment of the centipede's body has one pair of

   legs. _____

3. Frida slipped quietly through the darkness. All around her, forest creatures made night sounds that chilled her blood. Were there dragons lurking behind the trees? Would their fiery breath suddenly light up the night and scorch the earth?

   _____

Practice

▶ **Aim/Purpose and Audience**

Write a possible aim, purpose, and audience for each of the following:

4. A school report that compares and contrasts two subjects.

Aim: _____

Purpose: _____

Audience: _____

5. A short story about an imaginary world.

Aim: _____

Purpose: _____

Audience: _____

6. A poster on the school bulletin board about an upcoming school event.

Aim: _____

Purpose: _____

Audience: _____

7. An email message about everything that happened to you today.

Aim: _____

Purpose: _____

Audience: _____

WRITER'S CRAFT

UNIT 2 Ancient Civilizations • **Lesson 4** *The People on the Beach*

Prepositions and Prepositional Phrases

A preposition is a word that shows the relationship of a noun or pronoun to another word in a sentence.

Rule

▶ A preposition can be one word or more than one word.

▶ A **prepositional phrase** is a group of words that begins with a preposition and ends with a noun or pronoun, which is called the **object of the preposition.**

▶ The object of a preposition can be compound.

▶ A sentence can have more than one prepositional phrase.

Example

▶ The Zambezi River is **in** Africa. Zambia's copper industry thrives **because of** the Kariba Dam.

▶ The waters of the Zambezi River plunge **over the spectacular Victoria Falls.** (*Victoria Falls* is the object of the preposition *over.*)

▶ The upper part of the river flows **through Zambia and Angola.**

▶ The source **of the river** is approximately 4,800 feet **above sea level.**

Circle the preposition and underline the prepositional phrase in each sentence.

1. Did you know that many volcanoes are on islands?

2. Many islands that have volcanoes are in the Pacific Ocean.

3. A major volcanic zone extends around the Pacific Ocean.

4. The zone goes through New Zealand, the Philippines, Japan, and Alaska.

5. It also extends along North and South America's western coasts.

6. Located near the Mediterranean Sea is another major volcanic zone.

7. This zone extends across Asia.

8. Many countries in this zone have experienced volcanic eruptions.

9. Along the Atlantic Ocean runs the third major volcanic zone.

10. Many volcanic islands exist within this zone.

Prepositions and Prepositional Phrases

Practice

Underline each preposition once and each object of the preposition twice.

11. Florida is a peninsula on the southeastern coast of North America.

12. The capital of Florida is Tallahassee.

13. Florida is known for its sunny beaches.

14. The state produces a large amount of citrus fruit.

15. Tourists come to Florida because of its warm weather.

16. Alabama and Georgia border Florida to the north.

17. Along the western coast of Florida are many beaches.

18. On Florida's eastern coast is the Atlantic Ocean.

19. A group of islands, called the Florida Keys, extends from the southern tip of the peninsula.

20. Beyond the keys, to the south, lies the country of Cuba.

Proofread

Write the correct preposition above each underlined preposition.

The Food Guide Pyramid lists the nutrients needed <u>on</u> a nutritious diet. The guide was developed <u>from</u> the U.S. Department of Agriculture. The foods at the bottom <u>upon</u> the pyramid should be the biggest part of a nutritious diet. The bread, cereal, rice, and pasta group is <u>off</u> the bottom of the pyramid. Just <u>around</u> this bottom group is the fruit and vegetable group. Foods <u>by</u> this group are a major source of vitamins and minerals. <u>In front of</u> this group is the meat and dairy group. <u>In</u> the top of the pyramid is the fats and oils group. The foods <u>near</u> this group have the most calories. The Food Guide Pyramid can be used as a guideline <u>because of</u> a nutritious diet.

Name _____ Date _____

Telling in Time Order

▶ There are many kinds of writing in which the sequence, or order of events, is important. Stories, for example, wouldn't make sense if we didn't know what happened when. A set of directions for an activity would be impossible to follow. Time and order words are necessary for explaining a sequence. Here are some words that show the time and order of events. There are, of course, many more words of this kind.

then	morning	now	since	once
after	first	night	day	meanwhile
again	still	second	suddenly	week
finally	later	next	third	awhile
before	when	until	immediately	beginning

 **Try It!** **Underline the time and order words in each sentence.**

1. Once there were four sisters.

2. They had been very good friends from the beginning of their lives.

3. Gradually, though, things began to change.

4. First, the oldest sister began to find new friends at school.

5. The almost oldest sister then started dance classes and didn't think of anything else.

6. The almost youngest sister suddenly decided she wanted to be an astronomer.

7. She spent all evening at her telescope and sat all day writing numbers.

8. The youngest sister, meanwhile, began to feel very lonely.

9. After trying to talk to the oldest, the almost oldest, and the almost youngest sisters, she went to their mother.

10. "I want it to be the way it was before," she said sadly.

11. "Don't worry," said her mother. "They're still your friends, and they'll always be your sisters."

UNIT 2 Ancient Civilizations • **Lesson 4** *The People on the Beach*

▶ **Telling in Time Order**

Practice

Fill the blanks in the following sentences with time and order words to make the sequence clear.

12. _____ I got home from school, I changed clothes and went out to play.

13. My family enjoys having conversations _____ we are eating dinner.

14. New Year's Eve is the _____ day of the year.

15. I was waiting for two hours before Kim _____ got there.

16. I've been playing the piano _____ I was five years old.

17. When I got up this _____, the sun was shining brightly.

18. Did you spill the orange juice _____? That's twice this week.

19. Which of these recipes shall I try _____?

20. You have _____ four o'clock to finish your project.

21. Come here _____!

22. At _____, I try to finish two chapters of my book before I go to sleep.

23. James was the _____ person in line, just behind Brittany and Chase.

WRITER'S CRAFT

Quotation Marks and Underlining

Use quotation marks to enclose the titles of some types of literary works and to set off direct quotes. Underline other types of literary works.

Rule	**Example**
▶ Use quotation marks to show a person's exact words. If the quotation is divided, enclose both parts with quotation marks.	▶ "Benjamin Franklin invented bifocal lenses," our teacher said. "He also," she added, "established the University of Pennsylvania."
▶ Use quotation marks for titles of short stories, poems, articles, and book chapters.	▶ "The Necklace" (short story) "Presidential Race Too Close to Call" (article)
▶ Underline the titles of books, movies, magazines, and newspapers. In print, italics are used more often than underlining.	▶ The Adventures of Tom Sawyer (book) *The Wall Street Journal* (newspaper)

Add quotation marks or underlining to each item.

1. The Washington Post (newspaper)

2. A River Runs Through It (movie)

3. The Ranches of Texas (article)

4. To Build a Fire (short story)

5. Finding Least Common Multiples (book chapter)

6. The Call of the Wild (book)

7. The Smithsonian (magazine)

8. Fire and Ice (poem)

9. The Last of the Mohicans (book)

10. The Overcoat (short story)

UNIT 2 Ancient Civilizations • **Lesson 5** *The Riddle of the Rosetta Stone*

Quotation Marks and Underlining

Practice

Add quotation marks, underlining, or both to each sentence.

11. The Fire Builder is a chapter from the book Hatchet.

12. The New Search for Life on Mars appeared in the December 6, 1999, issue of Newsweek magazine.

13. Edgar Allan Poe's eighth book, Tales, includes the stories The Black Cat and The Purloined Letter.

14. Poe was a literary critic for a magazine called The New York Mirror.

15. Our unit test in science covered the chapters The Plant Kingdom and Origins of Life.

Proofread

Add quotation marks or underlining to the following dialogue.

Jason asked, Do you know what our English assignment is?

Yes, Jessica said, it's King Arthur and His Knights. She added, We're going to talk about the first chapter tomorrow in class.

Have you read the chapter yet? asked Jason.

Jessica replied, Yes, I read it last night. I think I'm going to like this book even better than Alice in Wonderland.

Really? Jason said. Do you think you'll like it better than Anne of Green Gables?

Well, said Jessica, that book will probably always be my favorite.

MECHANICS

Outlining

Writers use **outlines** to arrange their information into main topics and subjects.

Rule

▶ Main topics are capitalized and indicated by a Roman numeral.

▶ There are always at least two subtopics below a main topic. The first level of subtopics is indicated by a capital letter. The next level is indicated by an Arabic numeral. The first word in each subtopic is capitalized.

Example

▶ Whirlpools
   I. Kinds of Whirlpools

▶ I. Kinds of Whirlpools
   A. Where whirlpools occur
      1. Oceans
      2. Rivers
      3. Lakes

 **Try It!**   **Add Roman numerals, capital letters, and Arabic numerals to the following outline. Draw three lines under each letter that should be capitalized.**

Frogs

____ types of frogs

      ____ frogs who live in water

      ____ frogs who live on land

            ____ thin-skinned frogs

            ____ toads

____ physical characteristics

      ____ bodies

      ____ skin

      ____ legs

      ____ lungs

      ____ heads

            ____ eyes

            ____ ears

            ____ voice boxes

UNIT 2 Ancient Civilizations • **Lesson 5** *The Riddle of the Rosetta Stone*

Practice

Make an outline out of the following notes. The notes are already in the correct order.

Popular Fiction

Types of popular fiction
Science fiction
Mysteries
Historical fiction
Outlets for popular fiction
Books
Hardcover
Paperbacks
Magazines
Audio books
Film and television
Major motion pictures
Series television

WRITER'S CRAFT

Name _____ Date _____

Supporting Details

Supporting details include facts, reasons, and examples that support
your main point or topic sentence.

Rule	**Example**
▶ Use facts to support the main idea.	▶ Malgorzata "Margo" Dydek had a hard time as a young girl. Born in Poland in 1974, she was always the tallest kid in her class.
▶ Provide reasons why the main idea is true.	▶ Frequent teasing about her height gave Margo a low sense of self-worth.
▶ Use specific examples to support the main idea.	▶ Then she started playing basketball and everything changed. In 1999, she was named MVP at the European Basketball Championships.

 **Try It!** **Read the topic sentence below. Then add supporting sentences from the provided list. Add them in the order that makes the most sense.**

Boris Karloff was a respected actor who became almost a joke.

_____

_____

_____

_____

_____

- Clearly, he deserved more respect.
- Then, in 1931, he was cast as the monster in the film *Frankenstein.*
- In both England and Canada, he became known as a fine character actor with a beautiful speaking voice.
- He was born William Henry Pratt in England in 1887.
- He became rich and famous, but his name became a comedian's punch line.
- From that time on, he was typecast in monster and villain roles.

Comprehension and Language Arts Skills

UNIT 2 Ancient Civilizations • **Lesson 5** *The Riddle of the Rosetta Stone*

Practice

Read each of the following topic sentences. Then write three supporting details for the main idea.

1. Main Idea: Friends are an important part of life.

Supporting detail: _____

_____

Supporting detail: _____

_____

Supporting detail: _____

_____

2. Main Idea: Summer is a great time of year.

Supporting detail: _____

_____

Supporting detail: _____

_____

Supporting detail: _____

_____

3. Main Idea: Different heritages make America a rich culture.

Supporting detail: _____

_____

Supporting detail: _____

_____

Supporting detail: _____

_____

WRITER'S CRAFT

Fact and Opinion

Focus Writers convey information through facts and opinions.
Distinguishing fact from opinion helps readers fully understand what
they read.

> ▶ **Facts** can be proven by reliable sources such as dictionaries,
>   encyclopedias, and almanacs.
> ▶ **Opinions** are personal beliefs, not something that can be proven by
>   reliable sources.

Identify

Look through "His Majesty, Queen Hatshepsut." Some statements
the narrator makes are facts and some are opinions. Give two
examples of each.

1. Page: _____

  Fact: _____

  _____

2. Page: _____

  Fact: _____

  _____

3. Page: _____

  Opinion: _____

  _____

  _____

4. Page: _____

  Opinion: _____

  _____

  _____

UNIT 2 Ancient Civilizations • **Lesson 6** *His Majesty, Queen Hatshepsut*

▶ Fact and Opinion

Practice

Read each statement and tell whether it is a fact
or an opinion.

1. Apples are the best-tasting fruit. _____

2. A bicycle has two wheels. _____

3. Fish live in the water. _____

4. Sports are exciting for everyone. _____

5. The price on the menu is two dollars. _____

6. Rain can ruin everyone's good time. _____

7. My mother was born in Japan. _____

8. Blood flows through your veins. _____

Apply

Write a paragraph about ancient Eygpt. Make sure it contains both
facts and opinions.

_____

_____

_____

_____

_____

_____

_____

_____

_____

_____

_____

COMPREHENSION

Linking Verbs, Predicate Nouns, and Predicate Adjectives

A linking verb links the subject to a noun or adjective in the predicate. A predicate noun tells what the subject is. A predicate adjective tells about the subject.

Rule	**Example**
▶ Forms of the verb *be* are commonly used as linking verbs.	▶ A frog **is** an amphibian. Many frogs **are** green.
▶ Other common linking verbs are *seem*, *appear*, *look*, and *become*. Substitute a form of *be* to make sure a verb is a linking verb.	▶ Tadpoles become frogs. (Tadpoles will be frogs.)
▶ A **predicate noun** is a noun that follows a linking verb. It identifies or renames the subject.	▶ Chameleons are **lizards.**
▶ A **predicate adjective** is an adjective that follows a linking verb. It describes the subject.	▶ Their skin is **rough.**
▶ Predicate nouns and predicate adjectives may be compound.	▶ Crocodiles are **reptiles and carnivores.** Worms are **slow and slimy.**

Circle the linking verbs in the following passage.

Colors express different moods in art. The three primary colors are red, yellow, and blue. It is impossible to make these colors by mixing other colors. The secondary colors are orange, violet, and green. Each secondary color is a mixture of two primary colors. Value is the lightness or darkness of a color. If you add white to a color, it appears lighter. If you add black, the color seems darker. When the value of a color is lighter, the color is a tint. When the value of a color is darker, the color is a shade.

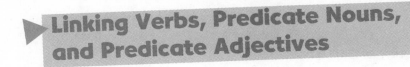

Linking Verbs, Predicate Nouns, and Predicate Adjectives

Practice

Circle the linking verb in each sentence. Underline the predicate nouns once and the predicate adjectives twice.

1. Phlox are tubular flowers native to America.

2. They smell sweet and fragrant in the spring.

3. White, purple, pink, and blue are their common colors.

4. Through the years, the shapes of some phlox petals became starlike.

5. Summer phlox seem content to grow in rich, moist soil.

6. Varieties of the rose and the phlox are domestic and wild.

7. A rose is a perennial shrub and a native of Asia.

8. The floral cup of a rose plant tastes berrylike.

9. The hybrid tea rose is the best-known type of rose.

10. Both phlox and roses remain popular among garden growers.

Proofread

Rewrite the passage in the space below. Combine every two sentences to form a sentence that contains either two predicate nouns or two predicate adjectives.

Zora Neale Hurston was a writer. She was an anthropologist who collected folklore. As a young woman, she was studious. She was successful in college. One of her well-known novels is *Mules and Men*. Another one of her well-known novels is *Dust Tracks on a Road*. In her later years, she became conservative. She became somewhat estranged from her fellow African Americans.

_____

_____

_____

_____

_____

_____

Comprehension and Language Arts Skills

GRAMMAR AND USAGE

UNIT 2 Ancient Civilizations • **Lesson 6** *His Majesty, Queen Hatshepsut*

Citing Sources

A **bibliography** is an alphabetical list of the sources you used in your research. Each source that is listed is called an entry, or **citation.**

Rule

▶ For a book, start with the author's last name. If there is a second author, start with his or her first name. Then include the title, underlined or italicized. Finally, include the publication information, using a comma to separate the publisher from the date of publication. Follow all three parts of your citation with a period.

▶ For a magazine or encyclopedia article, begin with the author's last name. Then include the title in quotation marks. Underline or italicize the title of the magazine or encyclopedia and add the date of publication and the page numbers. Separate the date and the page numbers with a colon. Follow all three parts of your citation with a period.

Example

▶ Unwin, Liam P., and Joseph Galloway. *Peace in Ireland.* Boston: Stronghope Press, 1990.

▶ Trefil, James. "When the Earth Froze." *Smithsonian,* December 1999: pp. 28–30.

Read each citation below. Then underline the part of the citation indicated in parentheses.

1. Brumbeau, Jeff. The Quiltmaker's Gift. Duluth, MN: Pfeifer-Hamilton Publishers, 2000. (date of publication)

2. Nichol, Barbara. Beethoven Lives Upstairs. New York: Orchard Books, 1993. (title)

3. Chait, Jonathan. "Color-Blind." The New Republic, March 12, 2001: pp. 16-17. (author)

4. Stewig, John Warren. King Midas. New York: Holiday House, 1999. (publisher)

5. Schiff, Bennett. "An Oasis of Art." *Smithsonian,* January 2001: pp. 74-81. (title of journal)

UNIT 2 Ancient Civilizations • **Lesson 6** *His Majesty, Queen Hatshepsut*

Write the following sources as they would appear in a bibliography.

6. The book entitled *On Writing Well* by William Zinsser was published in 1990 by HarperCollins Publishers in New York.

_____

_____

_____

7. A magazine article entitled "Betting on Designer Genes" was written by Jeff Wheelwright. It appears in the January 2001 edition of *Smithsonian* magazine on pages 29 to 36.

_____

_____

_____

8. Lawrence F. Kaplan wrote an article for the March 12, 2001, issue of The New Republic magazine. It's entitled "Offensive Line" and it's on pages 20 to 25.

_____

_____

_____

9. Ann E. Healy and Martha Walusayi are the coauthors of a book entitled Strategies for Writing: A Basic Approach. The book was published in 1997 in Lincolnwood, Illinois, by NTC Publishing Group.

_____

_____

_____

UNIT 2 Ancient Civilizations • **Lesson 7** *The Silk Route*

Review

Kinds of Sentences

Add the correct end punctuation to each sentence.

1. Did you know that Kilauea, in Hawaii, is the most active volcano on

   Earth _____

2. Kilauea has been continually erupting since 1983 _____

3. People still live in homes near the volcano _____

4. That's amazing _____

5. Find out more about Kilauea _____

Adjectives and Adverbs

Underline the adjectives once and draw an arrow from each adjective to the noun or pronoun it modifies. Underline the adverbs twice and draw an arrow from each adverb to the verb, adjective, or adverb it modifies.

6. Philip, the powerful king of Macedonia, controlled Greece in 338 B.C.

7. However, he had even grander dreams.

8. Philip planned to conquer the huge empire of Persia.

9. He died suddenly before he could achieve this goal.

10. Philip's son, Alexander, was very young when he became the emperor of Greece.

11. Alexander was destined to become one of the most successful leaders of all time.

12. His empire soon became even greater than his father's empire.

13. Alexander quickly moved his forces from Europe to Asia Minor.

14. Once he had conquered Persia, the restless, young emperor marched to India.

15. Alexander's soldiers always fought well, and they never lost a battle.

Prepositions and Prepositional Phrases ▶ Review

Underline each preposition once and each object of the preposition twice.

16. The empire of Alexander the Great extended over 1.5 million square miles of land.

17. Alexander began his march in Macedonia, near the Aegean Sea, and ended it on the banks of the Indus River.

18. He led his army of soldiers through Greece, into Africa, across Asia Minor, and into India.

19. Across his new empire, Alexander founded many new cities; most were named after him.

20. The greatest of these was Alexandria, Egypt, located on the shores of the Mediterranean Sea.

Linking Verbs, Predicate Nouns and Predicate Adjectives

Circle the linking verbs. Underline the predicate nouns once and the predicate adjectives twice.

21. Snakes are reptiles that have scaly skins.

22. The bodies of snakes appear long and tubular.

23. Snakes seem dangerous to many people.

24. A cobra is a highly venomous snake.

25. However, the majority of snakes are harmless to humans.

Quotation Marks and Underlining

Add quotation marks, underlining, or both to each sentence.

26. The Chicago Tribune, The Washington Post, and The New York Times sell more than a million copies each day.

27. I enjoyed an article in National Geographic called Bugging Out.

28. In addition to his novels The Call of the Wild and The Sea-Wolf, Jack London also wrote the popular short story To Build a Fire.

GRAMMAR, USAGE, AND MECHANICS

Passive Voice

The **voice** of a verb indicates whether the subject of a sentence performs the action of the verb or receives the action.

Rule

▶ A verb can be in the active or passive voice.

▶ In the first sentence, the subject is Jackie. He *does* something. He throws the ball. In the second sentence, the subject is the ball. It has something *done to it*. It is thrown.

▶ Generally, the active voice is simple, more direct, and more effective. However, there are times when the passive voice is appropriate. Sometimes you want to emphasize the receiver of the action. Sometimes the performer of the action is unknown.

▶ In general, it is best to avoid the passive voice in your writing.

Example

▶ Jackie threw the ball. (active voice)
The ball was thrown by Jackie. (passive voice)

▶ That building was built by unpaid laborers during the thirteenth century.

▶ Gold has been highly valued for thousands of years.

 **Read each sentence below and identify it as active or passive. Write an A for active or a P for passive.**

1. My mother bought that painting at least ten years ago. _____

2. It had been placed in a shop window near her office. _____

3. Every day, she passed the window on her way to work. _____

4. The painting seemed to call to her. _____

5. One day, she got good news. _____

6. A small raise had been owed to her for six months. _____

7. A check for an extra $120 was placed in her pay envelope. _____

8. Right after work, she rushed to the shop nearby. _____

9. A moment later, the painting was taken from the window. _____

10. Mother brought it home and hung it right over the mantle. _____

 **UNIT 2** Ancient Civilizations • **Lesson 7** *The Silk Route*

▶ Passive Voice

Practice

Change the sentences below from the passive to the active voice.

11. "Happy Birthday" was sung in outer space by Apollo IX astronauts on March 8, 1969.

   _____

   _____

12. Oklahoma is hit by more tornadoes than any other state.

   _____

   _____

13. About one quarter-pound of salt is contained in every gallon of seawater.

   _____

   _____

14. The Empire State Building in New York is hit by lightning about 500 times a year.

   _____

   _____

15. The seaside town of Sweetwater was lived in by comic strip hero Popeye the Sailor.

   _____

   _____

16. "The Star-Spangled Banner" is ranked the most difficult national anthem on Earth to sing by music experts.

   _____

   _____

WRITER'S CRAFT

UNIT 3 Taking a Stand • **Lesson 1** *The Pretty Pennies Picket*

Helping Verbs and Double Negatives

A helping verb helps the main verb tell about an action or a state of being.
A double negative is the use of two negative words to express the same idea.

Rule

▶ A helping verb helps the main verb express action or make a statement.

▶ The most common helping verbs are forms of *be*, *have*, and *do*.

▶ Many double negatives include a helping verb that is part of a contraction, such as *don't* or *can't*. Correct most double negatives by removing one of the negative words or by replacing one of the negative words with an affirmative word.

Example

▶ Many Americans **have** visited Washington, D.C.

▶ We **are** going there next month. **Do** you want to come along?

▶ I have**n't never** been to Washington, D.C. (incorrect)
I have **never** been to Washington, D.C. (correct)
I have**n't** ever been to Washington, D.C. (correct)

Circle all of the helping verbs.

The *Mona Lisa* is among the most famous paintings in the world. It was painted by the Italian artist Leonardo da Vinci. Da Vinci had just finished his painting *Last Supper* when he was asked to paint Mona Lisa del Giocondo. While he was painting her, da Vinci was invited to France by King Francis. The two men had met in Milan, where da Vinci was living. Da Vinci did not want to remain in Italy, so he accepted the French king's invitation. He took the *Mona Lisa* with him. A few years later, Da Vinci died in France. This is why the *Mona Lisa* is hanging in the Louvre, France's national museum.

Comprehension and Language Arts Skills

UNIT 3 Taking a Stand • **Lesson 1** *The Pretty Pennies Picket*

Helping Verbs and Double Negatives

Practice

Rewrite each sentence so that it includes a helping verb before each underlined verb. Do not change the form of the underlined verb.

1. I <u>played</u> baseball.

_____

2. I <u>catch</u> the baseball.

_____

3. We <u>played</u> baseball in my old neighborhood.

_____

4. With the other team <u>waiting</u> for us on the field, we warmed up.

_____

_____

5. <u>Waiting</u> for the field to dry after the rain, we often <u>played</u> catch.

_____

_____

Proofread

Correct any double negatives in the following paragraph.

Baseball isn't really not a new sport. A form of baseball was played in the United States as long ago as the 1700s. However, nobody never called it baseball back then. In New York City, one early form of baseball was called "one old cat." By 1835, baseball games called "town ball" and "New York ball" were played in large eastern cities. These games didn't have no bases like the ones that are used today. Instead, stakes were pounded into the ground to mark the "stations," as they were called back then. The players probably didn't never like the stakes because they could cause injuries. Stones had replaced the stakes by about 1840. However, the stones weren't never popular either. Somebody had the idea of using sand-filled sacks, which replaced the stones.

GRAMMAR AND USAGE

UNIT 3 Taking a Stand • **Lesson I** *The Pretty Pennies Picket*

Tone of a Business Letter

▶ A business letter is written to a person, company, or organization that you do not know personally. In a business letter, you may ask for information, complain about a product or service, or express a concern. When writing a business letter, be brief and concise. Explain the reason for your letter in the first sentence or two.

▶ A business letter should follow the correct form and should include all the appropriate parts: heading, inside address, salutation, body, closing, and signature.

▶ The tone of a business letter should be polite but not stiff, and friendly but not overly casual. The body of a business letter should sound more like a conversation than a textbook, but it should not be too informal.

Try It!

Revise the following sentences to make them more appropriate for a business letter. Some sentences need to be shorter and more to the point. Others need to be more polite and professional.

1. This letter is written for the purpose of requesting a brochure.

_____

_____

2. I tried your new cereal this morning, and I did not like it at all.

_____

_____

3. Send me the information I requested immediately.

_____

_____

4. I am writing to complain about the awful service at your restaurant last week.

_____

_____

UNIT 3 Taking a Stand • **Lesson I** *The Pretty Pennies Picket*

▶ **Tone of a Business Letter**

Practice

Choose one of the following topics and write the body of a business letter. Concentrate on using the proper tone in your business letter.

▶ request information from Mrs. Jones for a research project
▶ complain to Mr. Smith about a defective product

Dear _____

_____

_____

_____

_____

_____

_____

_____

_____

_____

_____

_____

_____

_____

_____

_____

_____

_____

_____

WRITER'S CRAFT

UNIT 3 Taking a Stand • **Lesson 2** *Class Discussion*

Making Inferences

Focus Good readers make inferences about characters and events as they read.

> ▶ An **inference** is based on information from the story and on personal experience and knowledge.

Identify

Look through "Class Discussion." Make two inferences about an issue, an event, or a character in the story. List the information from the story used to make each inference.

1. Page: _____

Inference: _____

_____

_____

Information: _____

_____

_____

2. Page: _____

Inference: _____

_____

_____

Information: _____

_____

_____

UNIT 3 Taking a Stand • **Lesson 2** *Class Discussion*

▶ Making Inferences

Practice

Read the following paragraph. Then, write three inferences you can reasonably make based on the information in the paragraph.

The students were happy and relaxed. It was a beautiful Friday afternoon. The windows were wide open, and a soft breeze ruffled the papers on Ms. Calhoun's desk. Yet the teacher did not look happy.

"What's wrong, Ms. Calhoun?" Ramone asked.

"It's our principal, Mr. Morgan," Ms. Calhoun explained sadly. "The school board wants him to retire."

"But he's been here forever!" Jordan said. "He was principal when my mom was in school. He's great!"

The entire class grew quiet.

Inference: _____

_____

_____

_____

_____

Inference: _____

_____

_____

_____

_____

Inference: _____

_____

_____

_____

_____

COMPREHENSION

Clauses and Subordinating Conjunctions

A clause is a group of words that has a subject and a verb. A clause may or may not stand alone as a sentence.

Rule	**Example**
▶ A main clause has a subject and a predicate and expresses a complete thought.	▶ Harry S. Truman was our thirty-third president.
▶ A subordinate clause has a subject and a predicate but does not express a complete thought.	▶ who was a Democrat (*who* is the subject)
▶ An adjective clause is a subordinate clause that modifies a noun or pronoun. It is usually introduced by a relative pronoun such as *that* or *which*.	▶ Truman spent twelve years working on his parents' farm, **which was in Missouri.**
▶ An adverb clause is a subordinate clause that often modifies the verb in the main clause. It tells *how, when, where, why,* or *under what conditions* the action occurs. It is introduced by a subordinating conjunction such as *after, while,* and *because.*	▶ **Before he became president in 1945,** Truman was a senator from Missouri.

Underline the main clause of each sentence.

When the western part of America was still being explored, Missouri was the starting point to the West. Lewis and Clark, who were famous explorers of the West, began and ended their journey in St. Louis. After Lewis and Clark returned from their expedition, many pioneers went westward along the Santa Fe and Oregon Trails, which both started in Independence, Missouri. The Pony Express, which was a mail service provided by riders on horseback, also began its route in Missouri. Once the riders left St. Joseph, they were expected to reach San Francisco within eight days.

Clauses and Subordinating Conjunctions

Practice

Underline the main clauses once. Underline the subordinate clauses twice.

1. Christopher Columbus's four voyages, which he made between 1492 and 1504, changed the map of the known world.

2. When he made his first voyage, Columbus landed on an island in the Bahamas that he named San Salvador.

3. He then sailed to Cuba and Haiti, which he called Hispaniola, before he traveled back to Spain.

4. When he made his second voyage, Christopher Columbus returned to Hispaniola where he established a small colony.

5. Columbus sailed along the coast of South America when he made his third voyage.

Proofread

Underline each subordinate clause and write the noun or verb that it describes above the clause. Circle the subordinating conjunctions.

After Christopher Columbus made his voyages, many other Spanish explorers sailed to the Americas, which they called the New World. In 1502, Nicolas de Orlando and 2,500 others set up a permanent settlement on Hispaniola, where they established sugar cane and tobacco plantations. While Orlando was colonizing Hispaniola, Balboa established a settlement near Panama. During the next Spanish expedition, which was led by Hernan Cortés, the Spaniards destroyed the magnificent Aztec empire. Ten years after Cortés seized the treasures of the Aztecs, Francisco Pizarro destroyed the mighty empire that the Incas had built in Peru.

GRAMMAR AND USAGE

Transition Words

Good writers use signal words and phrases, called transitions, to help readers understand the connection between ideas in sentences and paragraphs. There are several different kinds of transitions.

▶ To show the **time** when events take place in your writing, use words and phrases such as *last week, today, earlier,* and *yesterday.*

▶ To show the **order** of events in a story, use words such as *first, next, finally,* and *last.*

▶ To show the **place or location** of events in a story, use words such as *behind, nearby, to the right,* and *next to.*

▶ To **compare and contrast** two items, use words and phrases such as *in contrast, however, similarly,* and *also.*

▶ To **summarize** the main ideas in your writing, use words and phrases such as *in conclusion, therefore, to summarize,* and *as a result* to tie the main points together.

For each of the following examples, underline the signal words that help clarify the connection between ideas.

1. Jenny and her parents vacationed in Europe last year. First they visited London for a week. She learned a lot about England's history from her tour of the Tower of London. Then they went to Paris for five days, and she and her parents had dinner at the restaurant in the Eiffel Tower.

2. The room at the top of the stairs has a bookcase. On the top shelf of the bookcase, there is a book containing the complete works of Shakespeare.

3. Our family reunion picnic in Florida was a disaster this year. First, my father got lost on the way to the picnic, and we arrived an hour late. Second, six of us were crammed in the hot car, and my brother kept kicking my leg. Third, it began to rain when we arrived at the reunion.

4. As Brian and Dan waited in line for movie tickets, Brian remembered that he left his wallet on his desk. After Brian returned home to get his wallet, he and Dan went to a later movie.

UNIT 3 Taking a Stand • **Lesson 2** *Class Discussion*

▶**Transition Words**

WRITER'S CRAFT

Practice

Insert a transition word or words in the blanks to help connect the ideas in the following paragraphs.

5. Sarah plans on doing some research to help her decide which car to

   buy. _____ she plans on taking test drives of cars she

   is interested in buying. _____ she plans on having our
   cousin, who is a mechanic, inspect the car to make sure it is in good
   shape.

6. _____ at camp, we took a hike through the woods.

   _____ we were walking back to camp, our counselor

   noticed that the sky was dark. _____ we heard the
   tornado sirens warning that a tornado had been spotted. We needed
   to find shelter soon.

7. Because she missed the bus, Olivia walked to school

   _____. She arrived _____ late and
   missed most of first period.

8. Australian shepherds resemble Border collies. _____,
   Australian shepherds are much bigger than Border collies.

   _____ Border collies, Australian shepherds are born
   without tails.

**Write a brief description of an action-filled event using transition
words. Use place and location words to describe vividly where
the action takes place. Use time and order words to tell when
and in what order the action takes place.**

_____

_____

_____

_____

_____

_____

UNIT 3 Taking a Stand • **Lesson 3** *The Grimké Sisters*

Participles and Participial Phrases

A participle is a verb form that can be used as an adjective to modify a noun or a pronoun. A participial phrase is a participle and the other words that complete its meaning.

Rule	**Example**
▶ Form a present participle by adding *-ing* to a verb.	▶ Their **cheering** fans celebrated the team's victory.
▶ Most past participles are formed by adding *-d* or *-ed* to a verb. Others have irregular forms.	▶ The **practiced** team easily defeated their opponents. The **broken** goal post was replaced during halftime.
▶ A participial phrase includes the participle and the words that complete its meaning.	▶ **Blocking the goal,** the goalkeeper won the game.
▶ A gerund is a verb form that ends in *-ing* and is used as a noun.	▶ **Running** is a common workout for soccer players.
▶ A gerund phrase includes a gerund and the words that complete its meaning.	▶ **Exercising regularly** is a good habit.

Circle the participles and underline the gerunds in the following sentences.

1. Doing extremely well in the 1999 World Cup, the U.S. team made it to the final.

2. The defeated Brazil team lost to the U.S.

3. Many Americans enjoyed watching the game on television.

4. The disciplined U.S. defense did not allow any Chinese goals.

5. Desperately wanting a goal, the U.S. could not score either.

6. Fortunately, playing well under pressure was a skill the U.S. team possessed.

UNIT 3 Taking a Stand • **Lesson 3** *The Grimké Sisters*

Participles and Participial Phrases

Practice

Underline the participles and participial phrases. Draw an arrow to the noun or pronoun that each participle or participial phrase modifies.

7. Going into the shootout, both teams were scoreless.

8. Neither one of the undefeated teams could win.

9. The U.S. women, taking control of the game, scored the first four shots.

10. Diving for the ball, Briana Scurry blocked a shot by Liu Ying of China.

11. The player taking the last shot was Brandi Chastain.

12. Stepping up to the ball, Chastain fired a hard shot.

13. The diving goalkeeper missed the ball by an inch.

Proofread

Add commas where they are needed in the following sentences. Then rewrite the sentences by changing the position of the participle or participial phrase.

14. Long before arriving at the U.S. World Cup final in 1999 the U.S. women's team made up its mind to win.

_____

_____

15. Rising early every morning the U.S. team practiced for hours.

_____

_____

16. Their coach worked on the team's skills focusing on defense.

_____

_____

GRAMMAR AND USAGE

Author's Point of View

Focus Writers choose which point of view they will use to tell their story. Sometimes they tell a story through the eyes of a character. Sometimes they use an outside narrator to tell the story.

> ▶ Sometimes writers tell stories in the **first person**, using the words of a character. First-person narration includes words such as *I*, *me*, and *our*.
>
> ▶ Other times writers tell stories in the **third person**, using the words of an outside narrator. Third-person narration includes words such as *he*, *she*, *him*, *her*, *they*, and *theirs*.

Identify

Look through "I Have a Dream." Find three sentences that contain clues to the author's point of view. Write them below. Then, write the clue words used in each sentence.

Page: _____

Sentence: _____

_____

Clue words: _____

Page: _____

Sentence: _____

_____

Clue words: _____

Page: _____

Sentence: _____

_____

Clue words: _____

Is the story in the first or third person? _____

UNIT 3 Taking a Stand • **Lesson 4** *I Have a Dream*

▶ **Author's Point of View**

Practice

For each selection, write whether the point of view is first person or third person.

1. I've been riding a bike since I was three. And I've never fallen off. Except once. And it wasn't my fault. How was I to know they planted a tree in the middle of my favorite bike trail?

   Point of view: _____

2. If it had not been raining, I would never have gone into the old McHealy place. I knew it was supposed to be haunted, but I was getting soaked.

   Point of view: _____

3. When Maggie Jones strapped on her guitar and walked on stage, she was transformed. She was no longer a shy sixth grader. She was a rock star.

   Point of view: _____

4. Juan and Tim worked in the library after school. Both boys liked to be around books. Especially old, dusty books with the smell of history on them.

   Point of view: _____

Apply

Choose one of the paragraphs above and rewrite it from another point of view.

_____

_____

_____

_____

_____

_____

_____

_____

COMPREHENSION

UNIT 3 Taking a Stand • **Lesson 4** *I Have a Dream*

Verb Tenses

The tense of a verb tells when the action takes place.

Rule	**Example**
▶ The present tense of a verb expresses action that happens regularly.	▶ I **visit** Puerto Rico every summer.
▶ For singular nouns and the pronouns *he*, *she*, and *it*, add *-s* or *-es* to the verb to make it present tense. The base form of the verb is used for all other subjects.	▶ My grandmother **lives** in Puerto Rico. She **makes** lace for various shops. Many people **buy** her lace.
▶ The past tense of a verb expresses action that already happened. Add *-d* or *-ed* to the base verb to form the past tense of most verbs.	▶ My grandmother **learned** this skill from her mother.
▶ The future tense of a verb expresses action that will happen in the future. Add the helping verb *will* before the main verb.	▶ I **will help** my grandmother next summer.

 **Try It!**

Write present, past, or future above each underlined verb.

1. Last summer I <u>learned</u> how to prepare some Puerto Rican dishes.

2. Puerto Rican cooking <u>combines</u> Carib, African, and Spanish ingredients.

3. I <u>will enjoy</u> the unique food of Puerto Rico.

4. Seeds brought from around the world many years ago <u>flourished</u> in Puerto Rico.

5. The national dish is a stew that <u>contains</u> meat, crab, or chicken.

6. On Sunday, I <u>will prepare</u> this stew for my family.

7. Most Puerto Rican cooks <u>serve</u> cold avocados with this dish.

8. I <u>will slice</u> the avocado into thin pieces.

UNIT 3   Taking a Stand • **Lesson 4** *I Have a Dream*

Practice

Circle the correct form of each verb in parentheses.

9. Today, some artists still (knot/knotted) ropes into hammocks.

10. Hammocks were unknown in Europe before the Spaniards (arrive/arrived) in the New World.

11. Hammocks probably (remained/will remain) favorite napping places for many people.

12. Artists also (construct/will construct) native instruments called cuatros.

13. A cuatro (sounded/sounds) somewhat like a mandolin.

Proofread

Rewrite each sentence using the past and future tenses of the main verb.

14. Many people visit Puerto Rico.

_____

_____

15. Tourists fill the streets of San Juan.

_____

_____

16. Artisans welcome the tourists to their shops.

_____

_____

17. The island receives heavy rainfall.

_____

_____

GRAMMAR AND USAGE

UNIT 3 Taking a Stand • **Lesson 5** *Gandhi*

Types of Sentences

A sentence is usually defined as a group of words that expresses a complete thought.

Rule

▶ A simple sentence contains one subject and one predicate.
▶ Subjects and predicates also may be compound.

▶ A compound sentence contains two or more main clauses often joined by a comma and a coordinating conjunction or by a semicolon.
▶ A complex sentence contains a main clause and one or more subordinate clauses.
▶ A compound-complex sentence contains more than one main clause and one or more subordinate clauses.

Example

▶ **Nevada extends** about 320 miles east to west.
▶ **Las Vegas** and **Reno** are Nevada's largest cities. (compound subject) Many people **visit** Las Vegas and **enjoy** its many attractions. (compound predicate)
▶ **Early explorers searched for a great river in Nevada,** but **they never found it.**

▶ **The river,** which many people believed flowed to the Pacific Ocean, **did not exist.**
▶ **Nevada is one of the nation's driest states,** but **Lake Mead,** which is east of Las Vegas, **could cover the state of New York with a foot of water.**

Underline the main clauses and identify the type of sentence.

1. The capital of Nevada is Carson City, but Las Vegas is the largest city

   in the state. _____

2. Lake Mead, which is near Las Vegas, is located at the southwestern

   corner of Nevada. _____

3. Lake Mead is very long; its shoreline stretches for 550 miles. _____

4. Finished in 1935, Hoover Dam is the largest dam in the U.S. _____

5. Great Basin National Park is located in the southern part of the Snake Mountains, and

   the park includes forests, limestone caves, and a glacier. _____

▶**Types of Sentences**

Practice

Identify each sentence as simple, compound, complex, or compound-complex.

6. Gold and silver are still mined in Nevada today. _____

7. Many tourists visit the casinos in Las Vegas, and they also enjoy the resorts of Lake Tahoe. _____

8. Lake Tahoe, which is the largest mountain lake in North America, is 1,640 feet deep. _____

9. Evergreen forests surround the lake, and its water is clear and pure because the lake is high in the mountains. _____

10. Lake Tahoe is in the Sierra Nevada, which forms the border between Nevada and California. _____

11. Because Nevada usually receives little rain, the soil, which can be very dry, is not good for farming. _____

12. There are unusual red sandstone formations in the Valley of Fire.

_____

Proofread

Replace any awkward conjunctions with ones that best complete each sentence. Some sentences may need commas.

Before Nevada was a state many settlers came to the land in search of silver. In 1862, Congress established the Nevada Territory but in 1864 Nevada became the thirty-sixth state. Nevada's population has grown over the last fifty years whereas it remains one of the nation's least populated states.

UNIT 3 Taking a Stand • **Lesson 5** *Gandhi*

Sentence Variety

Using sentences of different lengths adds variety to your writing. Adding variety to your writing makes it more interesting for your readers.

Rule	**Example**
▶ Combine short, choppy sentences to form compound, complex, or compound-complex sentences.	▶ Our rivers are dirty. We need to clean them up. Our rivers are dirty, **and** we need to clean them up. (compound sentence)
▶ Expand sentences by adding detail to make them clearer and more interesting.	▶ John was late. John was late for the movie because his car broke down on the highway.
▶ Use synonyms to help add variety and eliminate the repetition of words.	▶ I like spaghetti a lot and eat it often. I also like hamburgers. I like spaghetti a lot and eat it often. I also enjoy hamburgers.

 **In each of the following examples, combine the two shorter sentences into one sentence.**

1. We know we have to stop dumping sewage in our rivers. It costs a lot to build treatment plants.

   _____

2. A package was delivered for you. You were at the store.

   _____

For each of the following examples, add details to expand the sentences.

3. It was cold.

   _____

4. I want to go to college.

   _____

UNIT 3 Taking a Stand • **Lesson 5** *Gandhi*

Practice

In the following examples, practice writing sentences of various lengths.

5. Write a compound sentence.

_____

6. Write a compound-complex sentence.

_____

7. Write a sentence containing a prepositional phrase.

_____

8. Write a sentence containing a compound subject.

_____

The following paragraph contains sentences that lack variety and are choppy. Revise the sentences to make them more interesting.

The singer Pete Seeger has always sung about what he believes is best for our country. Sometimes he speaks about it, too. In the 1960s he began to worry about clean water. He started a campaign to clean up the Hudson River in New York. Seeger lived near the Hudson River. He loved it. Seeger traveled up and down the river. He traveled on a sailing sloop called the *Clearwater.* He sang and spoke about the river. People decided to start cleaning it up.

_____

_____

_____

_____

_____

_____

_____

_____

WRITER'S CRAFT

Sentence Variety

Cause and Effect

Focus Understanding the causes and effects of events helps readers comprehend the story they are reading.

> ▶ A **cause** is an event that brings about other events. It is the reason something happens.
>
> ▶ The events brought about are called **effects**. An effect can become the cause of other effects.
>
> ▶ Writer's often use signal words and phrases to identify cause-and-effect relationships. These words include *because, so, if, then, since, for, as a result, therefore,* and *for this reason.*

Identify

You may be better able to organize examples of cause-and-effect relationships by making a chart. Look through "Sweeping Pittsburgh Clean," and find examples of cause-and-effect relationships.

Effect happened	Cause
Elizabeth became a journalist	a newspaper column titled "What Girls Are Good For"

UNIT 3   Taking a Stand • **Lesson 6** *Sweeping Pittsburgh Clean*

▶ **Cause and Effect**

COMPREHENSION

Practice

Write a possible effect for each of the following sentences.

1. Jordan forgot his homework at home.

Effect: _____

_____

_____

2. Maria wanted to buy a present for her father.

Effect: _____

_____

_____

3. The leaves were falling off the trees.

Effect: _____

_____

_____

Apply

Write a short newspaper article on an issue that concerns you, and use cause-and-effect relationships to support your ideas. Include signal words to help readers understand the cause-and-effect relationships.

_____

_____

_____

_____

_____

_____

_____

UNIT 3 Taking a Stand • **Lesson 6** *Sweeping Pittsburgh Clean*

Reflexive, Intensive, and Demonstrative Pronouns

Reflexive, intensive, and demonstrative pronouns have different functions in a sentence.

Rule

▶ A reflexive pronoun ends with *-self* or *-selves* and directs the action of the verb back to the subject.

▶ An intensive pronoun also ends with *-self* or *-selves* and adds emphasis to a noun or a pronoun.

▶ A demonstrative pronoun points out something. *This* and *these* refer to things nearby. *That* and *those* refer to things at a distance.

Example

▶ In Abraham Lincoln's time, many people taught **themselves** how to read.

▶ Lincoln **himself** learned how to read on his own.

▶ **This** is an interesting book about Lincoln's younger years.

Try It!

After each sentence, write whether the underlined pronoun is reflexive, intensive, or demonstrative.

1. You should buy <u>yourself</u> a book about Abraham Lincoln. _____

2. <u>That</u> is one of the best books I've read about him. _____

3. Lincoln <u>himself</u> was a very good writer. _____

4. He wrote many of his speeches <u>himself</u>. _____

5. One of his speeches included the famous saying, "A house divided

   against <u>itself</u> cannot stand." _____

6. There are many stories of Lincoln's tragic childhood; have you heard

   any of <u>those</u>? _____

7. I will educate <u>myself</u> on Lincoln's role as president during the

   Civil War. _____

UNIT 3 Taking a Stand • **Lesson 6** *Sweeping Pittsburgh Clean*

Reflexive, Intensive, and Demonstrative Pronouns

Practice

Circle the pronoun in parentheses that correctly completes each sentence.

8. Our teacher asked us to do some research on Abraham Lincoln (ourself/ourselves).

9. I bought a book about Lincoln for (me/myself).

10. In 1860, (he/himself) was elected president of the United States.

11. (This/That) was a time when slavery existed in half of the states in the Union.

12. Frederick Douglass, who had (hisself/himself) been born a slave, spoke out against slavery in the North.

13. Lincoln believed that slavery (it/itself) was dividing the country.

Proofread

Replace the incorrect pronouns with ones that best complete each sentence.

The Civil War broke out in 1861 when eleven states declared theirselves a separate country. This country called themselves the Confederate States of America. They feared that the North's ideas would end slavery in the South. President Lincoln hisself opposed slavery. He saw the country dividing themselves over this issue. We, as a country, found itself engaged in the worst battle ever fought on American soil. Lincoln wrote the Emancipation Proclamation in 1862 and freed the slaves. These same former slaves were now being asked to help fight the South.

GRAMMAR AND USAGE

UNIT 3 Taking a Stand • **Lesson 6** *Sweeping Pittsburgh Clean*

Avoiding Wordiness

In good writing, the writer uses the minimum amount of words to express his or her thoughts. This helps keep the reader engaged.
▶ Cut out words and phrases that repeat rather than add meaning.
▶ Delete vague words such as *pretty*, *very*, *sort of*, and *a little*.
▶ Check for the phrases *there is*, *there are*, *there was*, and *there were*. They are not always needed.

In the space provided, revise the following sentences to eliminate wordiness.

1. You can learn to type with all ten fingers on the keyboard, including your thumbs.

   _____

2. Riding a bicycle is pretty easy, but sometimes it takes a little time to learn.

   _____

3. There are certain animals that sleep during the day and hunt at night.

   _____

4. It was terribly thoughtful of him to come visit me in the hospital.

   _____

5. The assignment was basically very easy.

   _____

6. Due to the fact that it was snowing, school was cancelled.

   _____

7. Last year, my aunt had a set of twins, and they are really very cute.

   _____

UNIT 3 Taking a Stand • **Lesson 6** *Sweeping Pittsburgh Clean*

Avoiding Wordiness

Practice

Revise the following paragraph to eliminate the unnecessary words.

Can you type with all ten fingers, or do you just hunt around the keyboard with two fingers, trying to find the next letter, number, or character you need? If you're just playing computer games, you only need one or two fingers. If you are doing word processing, you need to know how to use all ten fingers quickly. There is a touch-typing system in which you use the same eight keys as a sort of base for your four fingers on each hand. Then you reach up, down, or sideways to certain other keys that you strike with each finger. It takes practice, but once you learn how, you can type fast and hardly ever need to look at your fingers.

_____

_____

_____

_____

_____

_____

_____

_____

_____

WRITER'S CRAFT

UNIT 3 Taking a Stand • **Lesson 7** *A Passage to Freedom*

Review

Helping Verbs and Double Negatives

Circle the words in parentheses that correctly complete the sentences.

1. I haven't (ever/never) been to a dogsled race.

2. There isn't (no/any) race that compares to Alaska's Iditarod Trail Sled Dog Race.

3. Hasn't (nobody/anybody) invited you to go?

4. My friend and I (am planning/are planning) to go this year.

Clauses and Types of Sentences

Underline the main clauses. Then write whether each sentence is simple, compound, complex, or compound-complex. Circle the conjunction or relative pronoun if one is used.

5. Alaska, which is not suitable for farming, is covered with mountain ranges and glaciers, and it also has many forests and tundra plains.

   _____

6. The animals that live in Alaska include caribou, moose, walruses, sea otters, and polar bears.

   _____

7. Although Alaska makes most people think of snow and ice, the southeastern part of the state is nearly always rainy.

   _____

8. The winds from the Pacific Ocean are filled with moisture, and they drop about 200 inches of rain on the Alaska panhandle each year.

   _____

9. The weather is rarely sunny in the panhandle, but when the sun is shining, the people who live there often take the day off to enjoy it.

   _____

UNIT 3 Taking a Stand • **Lesson 7** *A Passage to Freedom*

▶ Participles and Participial Phrases

Underline each participle or participial phrase that acts as an adjective and draw an arrow to the word that it describes.

10. Buying Alaska from Russia, the U.S. paid about two cents per acre.

11. Many disapproving Americans protested the purchase of Alaska.

12. These Americans, calling Alaska an "icebox," thought that the land was worthless.

13. Becoming the forty-ninth state, Alaska joined the union in 1959.

14. The salmon industry was one of the first developed industries in the state.

▶ Verb Tenses

Write whether the verb is past, present, or future tense.

15. Alaska **makes** most of its money in the fishing industry. _____

16. Petroleum **was** first **discovered** there in 1917. _____

17. New ferry systems built along the coast **will increase** tourism. _____

18. Many Russians **opposed** the sale of Alaska. _____

19. My aunt **lives** in Juneau, the state capital. _____

▶ Reflexive, Intensive, and Demonstrative Pronouns

Circle the correct pronouns.

20. Native Alaskans have many ways of keeping (theirselves/ themselves) warm.

21. Jack London, who (hisself/himself) lived in Alaska, wrote many stories about life in the Yukon Territory.

22. According to (him/himself), this was a land of both beauty and hardship.

23. Alaska (themselves/itself) is known as "The Land of the Midnight Sun."

24. (That/This) was the name given to it by native Alaskans.

UNIT 4 Beyond the Notes • **Lesson I** *What Is an Orchestra?*

Classifying/Categorizing

Focus Writers sometimes arrange information in categories to make it easier for readers to understand the information. As they read, good readers classify information to help them understand and remember the information.

> ▶ To classify or categorize things means to compare them and put them into groups or categories.
> ▶ Putting things into categories can sometimes give you a different perspective of the things being categorized.

Identify

Look through "What Is an Orchestra?" and answer the questions.

How does the author use classifying and categorizing to arrange the story?

_____

_____

_____

_____

How do the categories make the selection easier to read and understand?

_____

_____

_____

Explain your answer.

_____

_____

_____

_____

UNIT 4 Beyond the Notes • **Lesson 1** *What Is an Orchestra?*

▶ **Classifying/Categorizing**

COMPREHENSION

Practice

Read and think about the items named in the box below. Arrange the items into three different categories. Name each category and write the items that belong in it. You may put items in more than one category.

Handel	opera	cello	symphony	flute
Beethoven	violin	chamber music	Mozart	piano

Category 1: _____

_____

_____

Category 2: _____

_____

_____

Category 3: _____

_____

_____

Apply

Look through magazines for articles on music topics. Find an article in which the author categorizes or classifies information. Write two sentences explaining how classifying or categorizing the information makes the article easier to understand.

_____

_____

_____

_____

_____

_____

Parentheses and Hyphens

Parentheses are used to add extra information to a sentence, and a hyphen is often used to form a compound adjective.

Rule
▶ Parentheses set off words that define or explain a word in a sentence.
▶ Parentheses enclose the birth and death dates of a person.
▶ A hyphen forms a compound adjective that comes before a noun. Capitalize all proper adjectives.

Example
▶ I think archaeology **(the study of ancient artifacts)** is very interesting.

▶ Mary Leakey **(1913–1996)** discovered several important fossils.
▶ An **English-born** archaeologist, she worked alongside her husband for many years.

Add parentheses and hyphens where needed.

1. Dr. Ortega, the world famous ecologist, spoke to our class about the need to protect the rain forests.

2. He presented many well documented facts about the destruction of the rain forests.

3. The temperature in a typical rain forest remains at about 25°C 77°F all year.

4. Sun starved vines twist themselves up to the tops of trees.

5. The flying dragon a type of lizard has movable ribs that expand like wings.

6. The giant atlas moth another animal that lives in the rain forest has light reflecting patches on its wings.

7. The wingspan of a giant atlas moth is about twelve inches thirty centimeters.

8. During the day, the moth hides itself in broad leaved plants.

▶ Parentheses and Hyphens

Practice

Cross out or correct any parentheses and hyphens if they are used incorrectly.

9. Marie Curie, 1867–1934, is the only woman who has ever won two Nobel prizes.

10. Her marriage to her husband (July 25,) 1895 marked the start of a partnership in chemistry that would affect the whole world.

11. She discovered polonium (named in honor of her native country, Poland in the summer of 1898.

12. Polonium is a silvery gray or black metallic element.

13. It is also highly-radioactive.

14. One use of polonium (an industrial use) is to eliminate static electricity in plastic factories.

15. Pierre (and Marie) Curie also discovered radium.

16. Radium containing paint was considered to be a health hazard in the 1930s.

17. In the past, radium was useful in the treatment-of-cancer.

Proofread

Correct the errors in the following paragraph by crossing out or adding parentheses and hyphens where they are needed.

Tropical rain forests, especially those in South America, are the most diverse habitats (on Earth). The rain forests are home to thousands of species of rare-plants and animals. Many rain forest animals live in the forest canopy the tops of trees, which are mainly broad leaved trees. The canopy is typically about 164 feet 50 meters above the ground. Some high-flying animals hunt among the treetops (for their prey), while others feed on the abundant-leaves and colorful-fruits of the canopy. A majority of what scientists believe to be the oldest flowering plants are found in rain forests especially tropical rain forests in parts of South America.

MECHANICS

UNIT 4 • Beyond the Notes • **Lesson I** *What Is an Orchestra?*

Sentence Elaboration and Expansion

When writing, think about what else your readers might need to know or like to know about your subject. Adding helpful details can better explain or describe the information in your sentences.

Rule

▶ Identify people, places, and terms in your sentences. An adjective clause, for example, can be useful.

▶ Add words that tell precisely where or when an event occurred.

▶ Add adjectives or descriptive phrases that help your readers form clear pictures and use their senses.

▶ Add details to make connections clearer, using words such as *because, since, so,* and *so that.*

Example

▶ The author **who wrote the book about Ancient China** came to our school last month to give a talk.

▶ My parents' anniversary party, **held last week,** was a lot of fun.

▶ **Through the heavy morning mist,** I could see my uncle's **majestic stone** castle perched on top of the hill.

▶ I was very eager to accept my uncle's invitation to visit, **since I had never been in a castle before.**

 **Try It!** **Read the following sentences and underline the details that help explain or describe the basic statement.**

1. The Mayas, who built one of the great civilizations of our ancient world, lived in what is now Guatemala and Mexico.

2. The Mayas constucted giant pyramids that towered above the jungles.

3. Although they had only stone tools, the Mayan artists created finely chiseled carvings.

4. Their civilization, which lasted from about 2000 B.C until A.D. 1697, ended when the last of their people were conquered by Spanish armies that followed the explorer Cortes.

5. The crumbling ruins of their cities still stand.

UNIT 4 Beyond the Notes • **Lesson 1** *What Is an Orchestra?*

Sentence Elaboration and Expansion

Practice

Rewrite the following sentences by adding details to better explain the information in each one. The words in parentheses tell which type of information to add.

6. Sara rides horses every week. (where)

_____

_____

7. She practices her riding skills each Saturday. (why)

_____

_____

8. Misty is her female horse. (describe Misty)

_____

_____

9. The equestrian event will take place soon. (when and where)

_____

_____

Find an example from your own writing that could be improved with details. Revise the paragraph or passage below.

_____

_____

_____

_____

_____

_____

_____

_____

WRITER'S CRAFT

Indefinite, Relative, and Interrogative Pronouns

Different pronouns can have different functions in a sentence.

Rule

▶ An indefinite pronoun refers to a general group of people, places, or things. Some of these include *another, each, much, no one,* and *someone.*

▶ A relative pronoun can be used to introduce an adjective clause. Some of these pronouns include *that, who, whom, which,* and *whose.*

▶ An interrogative pronoun introduces a question. Interrogative pronouns include *who, whom, which, what,* and *whose.*

Example

▶ **Anyone** can see that we need to protect pandas in the wild.

▶ The giant panda, **which** once roamed freely in China, is now an endangered species.

▶ **What** can be done to help them?

Write whether each underlined pronoun is an indefinite pronoun, a relative pronoun, or an interrogative pronoun.

1. <u>Who</u> told you that the red panda is actually a type of raccoon? _____

2. The red panda, <u>which</u> is also called the lesser panda, is much

   smaller than the giant panda. _____

3. <u>Someone</u> once told me that a giant panda eats thirty-three to

   sixty-six pounds of bamboo shoots a day. _____

4. <u>Which</u> type of panda sleeps during the day and eats at night? _____

5. A panda has an extra thumb, <u>which</u> it uses to grip bamboo stems.

   _____

Indefinite, Relative, and Interrogative Pronouns

Practice

Choose the pronoun that correctly completes each sentence and identify what kind it is.

6. (Everyone/Anyone) in our class will write a report about pandas.

    _____

7. (What/Which) type of panda interests you more, the giant panda or

    the lesser panda? _____

8. I have learned (anything/something) about pandas from reading

    about them. _____

9. (Where/Which) are the majority of pandas located today?

    _____

10. Giant pandas, (that/which) are used to living alone, are extremely

    shy and timid. _____

11. I'm not sure (that/what) the lesser panda eats. _____

12. (Whom/Who) could answer that question? _____

13. (Many/Much) pandas have thick, insulating fur. _____

Proofread

Correct the following paragraph by crossing out the incorrect pronouns and writing the correct pronouns above them.

The panda is just some of the exotic animals who live in Asia; other is

the tiger. The largest species of tiger is the Siberian tiger, that can grow

to be more than ten feet in length. A tiger has sharp claws and teeth,

which it uses to catch its prey. Some tigers inhabit grassy or swampy

areas, that they usually live alone. Another prefer the remains of

buildings such as courts and temples.

GRAMMAR AND USAGE

Name _____   Date _____

Organization of a Narrative Paragraph

▶ A narrative paragraph moves a story's plot along by answering the
question *what happened?* or by describing a character or setting.
When you write a narrative paragraph, first choose the important
events to include in your paragraph. Then, tell about these events in a
logical order.

▶ An effective way to organize ideas in a narrative paragraph is
chronological, or time, order. Use time and order words such as *next*,
late at night, tomorrow, and *last* to tell what happened first, second,
third, and so on. These transition words help readers keep track of the
events in your paragraph. Vary the transitions you use in your narrative
paragraph to make your writing lively.

 **Use the information below to write a narrative
paragraph, organizing the ideas in chronological order.**

1. Mr. Flores asked the class to settle down.

2. He handed out a flyer.

3. Lucas began folding the flyer into a paper airplane.

4. Julio knew that the information on the flyer was serious.

5. He was the class president and wanted to set a good example for the other students.

6. Mr. Flores announced that the school might be closing.

7. The class was silent.

_____

_____

_____

_____

_____

_____

Organization of a Narrative Paragraph

Practice

Read the following passage, and underline the time and order words that show the chronological order of the events.

This morning, I tossed all my clothes into my suitcase and strapped my bag closed. Then I dragged the bag to the hotel door. "I'm late," I cried to the manager. "I've overslept! I'm supposed to be on the 10:30 plane to Chicago, and it's already 10:05." I quickly hailed a taxi at the hotel gate, and we raced through the winding streets, just missing a bike messenger who was nearly thrown into a passing truck. Just three years earlier, on a rainy day in St. Louis, I had arrived hurriedly at the airport, only to see my plane take off as I stood helplessly at the gate. Today, I could not miss my plane.

Outline a narrative paragraph that you would like to write using chronological order.

_____

_____

_____

_____

_____

_____

_____

_____

_____

_____

_____

_____

_____

WRITER'S CRAFT

UNIT 4 Beyond the Notes • **Lesson 3** *Aïda*

Drawing Conclusions

Focus Good readers use information in the text to draw conclusions about characters and events in a story.

> ▶ Authors do not always provide complete and explicit descriptions of or information about characters and events in a story. Readers can use clues or suggestions provided by an author to draw conclusions about characters and events in a story.
> ▶ Conclusions are always supported by evidence from the text.

Identify

Look through "Aïda" for information that can be used to draw conclusions about the characters and events in the story. Write the conclusions drawn and the information from the text used to draw the conclusions.

1. Conclusion: _____

   _____

   Text evidence used to draw conclusion: _____

   _____

   _____

2. Conclusion: _____

   _____

   Text evidence used to draw conclusion: _____

   _____

   _____

3. Conclusion: _____

   _____

   Text evidence used to draw conclusion: _____

   _____

   _____

Name _____ Date _____

▶ **Drawing Conclusions**

Practice

Pick an interesting scene or event from "Aïda," and rewrite it in your own words. Include any conclusions drawn about the characters or events in this scene.

_____

_____

_____

_____

_____

_____

_____

_____

_____

_____

_____

_____

_____

_____

_____

_____

_____

_____

_____

_____

_____

COMPREHENSION

Appositives and Appositive Phrases

Appositives and appositive phrases identify nouns or add information to them.

Rule

▶ An appositive is a noun placed next to another noun to identify it or add information to it.

▶ An appositive phrase includes an appositive and the other words that modify it.

▶ No commas are needed if the appositive phrase is essential to the meaning of the sentence.

▶ If the appositive phrase is nonessential, the phrase should be set off with commas.

Example

▶ James Madison's wife, **Dolley,** was known as a good hostess.

▶ Thomas Jefferson, **our third president,** was a close friend of Madison.

▶ Jefferson appointed his friend **James Madison** as secretary of state.

▶ Madison, **one writer of the Constitution,** is known as the "Father of the Constitution."

Try It! Write *yes* if the underlined appositive or appositive phrase is essential. Write *no* if it is nonessential.

1. In 1797, a conflict developed between Thomas Jefferson, <u>the secretary of state at the time</u>, and Alexander Hamilton. _____

2. Secretary of the Treasury <u>Alexander Hamilton</u> wanted to strengthen the powers of the federal government. _____

3. James Madison sided with his friend <u>Thomas Jefferson</u>. _____

4. Together they formed an opposition party, <u>the Jeffersonian Republicans</u>. _____

5. The Jeffersonian Republicans became a major opponent of Hamilton's party, <u>the Federalists</u>. _____

UNIT 4 Beyond the Notes • **Lesson 3** *Aïda*

Appositives and Appositive Phrases

Practice

Underline each appositive and appositive phrase, and draw an arrow from each appositive or appositive phrase to the noun that it modifies.

6. James Madison grew up on Montpelier, a plantation in Virginia.

7. Madison was educated at the College of New Jersey, now called Princeton University.

8. In the year of the American Revolution, 1776, Madison was chosen to help draft the Virginia Constitution.

9. Along with two other prominent politicians, Alexander Hamilton and John Jay, Madison wrote a series of papers.

10. The papers were published in *The Federalist*, a series of eighty-five essays.

Proofread

Correct the following paragraph by crossing out the commas that are not needed for appositives and appositive phrases and adding commas where needed.

   The party formed by James Madison and his friend, Thomas Jefferson, was an early form of one of our present-day parties the Democratic Party. When Thomas Jefferson the leader of the Jeffersonian Republican Party was elected president in 1801, Americans showed their support for the rights of the states over a central authority the federal government. President Jefferson appointed his longtime supporter, James Madison, as his secretary of state. Eight years later, James Madison was elected president, and his running mate, George Clinton, became vice president. As president, Madison led the country through a major crisis the War of 1812.

GRAMMAR AND USAGE

Dialogue

Dialogue tells the story in a play. Each line of dialogue should tell something about the plot or the characters' actions, thoughts, and feelings. Use the following rules for writing dialogue in a play.

Rule	**Example**
▶ When a character speaks, write his or her name in capital letters followed by a colon. Begin the dialogue on the same line. Do not use quotation marks.	▶ ERIC: That's so unfair! (*Pointing to* Nathan) Why should I be grounded for something HE did?
▶ Stage directions tell how a character moves. They also describe a character's facial expressions. Stage directions should be italicized and set in parentheses. Characters' names should *not* be italicized.	▶ NATHAN: (*Frowning and standing with his hands on his hips*) He blames EVERYTHING on me, Mom!
▶ Make sure the way each character speaks matches his or her personality or mood. Use different sentence lengths and styles, as well as specific words that indicate a character's age group, level of education, or the time period in which he or she lives.	▶ ERIC: (*Angrily*) Get a grip, Nathan! You know that's not true!

Try It! **Add stage directions to the following lines of dialogue.**

SERGEANT: _____ Briggs! Follow me to that
         barricade! Stay low!

BRIGGS: Watch out Sergeant! _____ He's behind you!

ENEMY: _____ You men are on enemy territory now.

    You're going to have to come with me. _____

SERGEANT: _____ That may be true, but we won't
       go quietly.

▶ **Dialogue**

Practice

Read the following paragraph from a story. Then rewrite the paragraph as a scene in a play. Use the correct format for writing dialogue in a play and be sure to include stage directions.

"Hey, Kevin! I'm talking to you!" Alan persisted.

Kevin stopped walking and turned around. "What do you want?" he asked. His eyes blazed. "Do you want to gloat some more?"

"I didn't tell the coach! Honest!"

Kevin started walking. "You wanted me off the team. Now I am. End of story."

"Would you just please listen to me!" Alan shouted.

"Chris told the coach that you cheated on the science test."

"But I didn't cheat!" Kevin paused. "I was going to, but . . . I just thought that . . . oh, why am I talking to you?" He waved his hand in dismissal.

"Because you know I'm telling the truth." Alan nodded. "You believe me."

_____

_____

_____

_____

_____

_____

_____

_____

_____

_____

_____

WRITER'S CRAFT

Dashes and Colons

Dashes and colons clarify writing by showing where a pause should take place or by introducing a list.

Rule	**Example**
▶ A dash indicates a sentence break or a change in thought.	▶ The Appalachian Mountains—**one of Earth's oldest mountain ranges**—cover much of Pennsylvania.
▶ A dash indicates an interruption in someone's speech.	▶ "Did you see the new exhibit **—the one on Picasso**—at the Philadelphia Museum of Art?" asked Luther.
▶ A colon introduces a list of items at the end of a sentence. The words *these, the following*, or *as follows* usually come before a list.	▶ Pennsylvania contains many historic sites, such as the following: **Gettysburg National Military Park, Independence National Park, and Valley Forge National Park.**
▶ A colon is also used to introduce an important quote.	▶ Pennsylvania founder William Penn described the state as such: **"This land is the foundation of a free colony for all mankind."**

 **Add dashes or colons to the following sentences if they are needed.**

1. Charles II, the King of England, granted the land that later became Pennsylvania to William Penn in 1681.

2. During colonial times, Pennsylvania was settled by many ethnic groups, which included the following English, German, Scots-Irish, French, Welsh, Cornish, and Irish.

3. The Pennsylvania Dutch possibly my ancestors cleared large farms in the southeastern part of the state.

4. They raised cattle and grew corn, squash, and wheat.

5. Benjamin Franklin, a famous Pennsylvanian, coined some well-known sayings, including this one "Early to bed and early to rise, makes a man healthy, wealthy, and wise."

UNIT 4   Beyond the Notes • **Lesson 4** *The Sound of Flutes*

▶ **Dashes and Colons**

MECHANICS

Practice

Cross out unnecessary dashes and colons and add them where they are needed.

6. Pittsburgh which isn't the state capital lies on the Allegheny Plateau.

7. Hikers, fishers, and photographers are drawn to the plateau because of its natural formations, such as: fields, bogs, and streams.

8. The area is surrounded by forests that include: beech, birch, and maple trees.

9. The plateau features Fallingwater, a home on a waterfall—yes, a waterfall that was designed by Frank Lloyd Wright.

10. Edgar Kaufmann described Fallingwater with these words "Frank Lloyd Wright created it as a declaration that in nature man finds his spiritual as well as physical energies."

Proofread

Combine each pair of sentences into one sentence that includes a colon or dashes.

11. There are three major cities in Pennsylvania. They include Philadelphia, Pittsburgh, and Harrisburg.

    _____

    _____

12. Philadelphia was laid out in a grid in 1682. It was a new idea at the time.

    _____

    _____

13. Benjamin Franklin expressed his dislike for war. He once said, "There never was a good war or a bad peace."

    _____

    _____

UNIT 4 Beyond the Notes • **Lesson 4** *The Sound of Flutes*

Plot

> The chain of events in a story is called the plot. A well-developed plot will make your story easier for you to organize and write, and it will make it easier for your readers to understand.
>
> ▶ Every good story has a beginning, a middle, and an end.
> ▶ Introduce problems at the beginning of the story.
> ▶ In the middle of the story, the characters go through one or more conflicts as they try to solve the problem.
> ▶ The highest point of interest in the story takes place when the problem begins to be resolved. This is called the climax.
> ▶ After the climax, the conclusion occurs. The conclusion finishes telling how the problem is solved.

Try It! **You know the story of "Little Red Riding Hood." On the lines below, outline the plot of the story.**

Story: _____

_____

Character: _____

_____

Problem: _____

_____

Conflicts the character encounters: _____

_____

Resolution: _____

_____

UNIT 4 Beyond the Notes • **Lesson 4** *The Sound of Flutes*

WRITER'S CRAFT

Practice

Read the passage below and answer the questions that follow.

"We'll be back before lunch," said Matt. He slapped at the smooth brown water with his paddle. "No one will even know we're gone."

Matt was sitting in one of Camp Kanobi's wooden canoes. A sliver of the sun rose slowly over the green mountains. Matt planned to sneak off and explore the other side of the Longhorn River. He wanted his friend Scott to come with him.

Scott finally shrugged and climbed into the canoe. About halfway across the river, Matt noticed the boat was filling with water. He didn't say anything to Scott because he didn't want to scare him. He knew Scott wasn't a great swimmer. Before they reached the far shore, Scott turned around with a scared look on his face. There was no way around it. Their canoe was sinking fast.

1. Who are the main characters in this passage?

_____

2. What happens at the beginning of the passage?

_____

_____

3. What is the main problem that Matt and Scott face?

_____

Finish the story by writing a climax and a conclusion.

_____

_____

_____

_____

_____

_____

_____

UNIT 4   Beyond the Notes • **Lesson 4** *The Sound of Flutes*

Setting

If you want readers to picture the events in your stories, you need to create vivid settings.

▶ The setting of a story tells *when* the events take place. A story can be set in the past, the present, or the future.

▶ The setting of a story is also *where* the events take place. The setting may be general, such as a state or country, or specific, such as "a grocery store in Muncie, Indiana."

▶ A story may have more than one setting. Each new setting should be described so that the reader understands the change in time and place.

▶ The writer makes the setting interesting to the reader by describing how a place looks, sounds, feels, and smells.

 **Try It!**   **Read the following passage. Then answer the questions about setting.**

Once upon a time, a long, long time ago, there lived a poor farmer. The farmer and his wife had three daughters. All of their daughters were beautiful, but the middle daughter's beauty shone brighter than the sun.

Although they were desperately poor, the farmer and his family were content in their small farmhouse on the edge of a vast forest.

One cold night, after everyone had gone to bed, there came a rap at the door. Upon answering the door, the farmer jumped back in fright at the sight of a large brown bear huddled on the doorstep.

1. When does this story take place? _____

2. Which sentences or phrases provide details about the setting? _____

_____

3. How does the setting help to create a mood?_____

_____

▶ Setting

WRITER'S CRAFT

Practice

Write a paragraph describing the setting of a story you plan to write or a story that you have already written.

_____

_____

_____

_____

_____

_____

In order to help readers visualize what is happening in a story, authors often include information about setting. Record any details from a story you have read that helped you picture where and when the story took place.

Story title: _____

Setting: _____

How the setting is described: _____

_____

_____

How the description added to my understanding and enjoyment of the

story: _____

_____

_____

Name _____ Date _____

Characterization

> Characterization is the writer's way of revealing characters to readers.
> ▶ When writing, show the way a character acts.
> ▶ Show what the character says and how she or he says it. Try to use the same kinds of words that your character would use.
> ▶ Show what the character is thinking.
> ▶ Show how the character feels.
> ▶ Show how other characters react to or think about your characters.

Find two examples of characterization in stories you have read. Write the name of the character, and tell what the character thinks, says, or feels. Explain how this reflects the character's personality.

1. Character: _____

_____

What he or she thinks, says, or feels: _____

_____

How this reflects the character's personality: _____

_____

2. Character: _____

_____

What he or she thinks, says, or feels: _____

_____

How this reflects the character's personality: _____

_____

▶**Characterization**

Practice

Read the passage. Describe how the actions and thoughts of the two characters reflect their personalities.

Howie slouched into his seat on the bus. He hadn't made the basketball team again. This summer was a waste—running every morning at five, lifting weights until seven, then rushing to his summer job at the lumberyard. The coach had some nerve to tell him he was too slow.

"Hey, man," squeaked Charley. "Scoot over so I can sit next to you."

"I hear you didn't make the basketball team," Charley said. "Too bad. I didn't make it either. Oh well, more time to do other things, I say. Cheer up! I think I'll try out for wrestling. What about you? You'd be great!"

Howie glared at Charley.

3. What Howie's thoughts and actions tell about him:

_____

_____

4. What Charley's thoughts, words, and actions tell about him:

_____

_____

Write a dialogue between two characters from a story you have written that reflects their personalities.

_____

_____

_____

_____

_____

_____

_____

WRITER'S CRAFT

Cause and Effect

Focus Writers use cause-and-effect relationships to help the reader understand the connection between events in a story.

> ▶ A cause is why something happens. It is an event that brings about other events.
> ▶ An effect is what happens.
> ▶ Writers use signal words and phrases to identify cause-and-effect relationships. These words include *because, so, if, then, since, for, as a result, therefore,* and *for this reason.*

Practice

Read the following examples from "Ray and Mr. Pit," and identify the causes that brought about each effect.

1. Music was the only thing that Ray Charles was excited about as a child.

   Cause: _____

   _____

2. When Mr. Pit played the piano, Ray just stared at him.

   Cause: _____

   _____

3. Mr. Pit thought Ray loved music as much as he did.

   Cause: _____

   _____

4. Mr. Pit was always anxious to teach Ray something new about the piano.

   Cause: _____

   _____

Use the following signal words to describe a cause-and-effect relationship.

1. Since

Cause-and-Effect Relationship: _____

_____

2. Because

Cause-and-Effect Relationship: _____

_____

3. So

Cause-and-Effect Relationship: _____

_____

4. Then

Cause-and-Effect Relationship: _____

_____

5. As a result

Cause-and-Effect Relationship: _____

_____

Write a short paragraph about a talent that you have and a person who has inspired you. Use cause-and-effect relationships to describe your talent.

_____

_____

_____

_____

_____

_____

UNIT 4   **Beyond the Notes • Lesson 5** *Ray and Mr. Pit*

Fragments

A fragment does not express a complete thought, but it is often punctuated as a sentence.

Rule	**Example**
▶ A fragment may be missing a subject.	▶ Escaped to safety in the North.
▶ A fragment may be missing a predicate.	▶ Many African American slaves.
▶ A fragment may be missing a subject and a predicate.	▶ From the South.
▶ Correct a fragment by adding the missing sentence parts.	▶ Many African American slaves from the South escaped to safety in the North.

Write *fragment* or *sentence* next to each item.

1. Led hundreds of slaves to freedom. _____

2. Harriet Tubman escaped slavery. _____

3. Born a slave. _____

4. Known as "the Moses of her people." _____

5. Abolitionists opposed slavery. _____

6. They celebrated her courage. _____

7. The railroad's most famous conductor. _____

8. Tubman served as a scout and a spy. _____

9. Of former Abolitionist friends. _____

10. She housed orphans and the elderly. _____

UNIT 4   Beyond the Notes • **Lesson 5** *Ray and Mr. Pit*

Fragments

Practice

Write whether the following fragments are missing a subject, a predicate, or both.

11. Was a system in the northern states. _____

12. The Underground Railroad. _____

13. Was neither underground nor a railroad. _____

14. In the South. _____

15. The network of routes. _____

16. Former slave Harriet Tubman. _____

17. Of northerners participated. _____

18. As far north as Canada. _____

19. From 40,000 to 100,000. _____

20. Walked all the way. _____

Proofread

Use proofreading marks to correct the fragments in the paragraph below.

   Harriet Beecher Stowe wrote a story on slavery based on her reading of abolitionist writings. And on what she saw in Ohio and Kentucky. In 1852, the story appeared in book form as *Uncle Tom's Cabin.* The book was very popular with abolitionists. However, it was hated in the South. Where reading or even owning the book was dangerous. The book helped both pro- and antislavery sentiment. Some people thought *Uncle Tom's Cabin* was one of the causes of the Civil War. Because it contributed to the popular feeling against slavery.

GRAMMAR AND USAGE

Name _____ Date _____

Dialogue

When you write a story with more than one character, your story will seem more lively and realistic if you use dialogue to show the characters talking to each other. Dialogue helps keep readers interested, and it moves the action of the story along.

Use the following rules for writing dialogue correctly.

Rule

▶ Use quotation marks to set off a speaker's exact words. If the speaker is named before the quotation, put a comma before the opening quotation marks. The part of the sentence that names the speaker is called the **speaker tag**.

▶ Start each quotation with a capital letter. When the spoken part ends, put a punctuation mark inside the closing quotation marks.

▶ Begin a new paragraph with each new speaker.

Example

▶ "I need to go to the library," said Tory. "Could you drive me there?"
Her mother replied, "Sure, but you have to wait a few minutes while I get ready."

▶ "Hello," he said boldly, "how are you today?"

 **Try It!** **Rewrite each sentence as a quotation. Include a speaker tag.**

1. Vicky said that she needed help with her homework. _____

_____

2. George asked Vicky if she had a book about insects. _____

_____

3. Luis yelled that the washing machine was leaking. _____

_____

Name _____   Date _____

UNIT 4   Beyond the Notes • **Lesson 5** *Ray and Mr. Pit*

Practice

Read the paragraph and underline the speaker in each sentence.

"See you later, Mom," said Kevin, walking through the kitchen to the back door. Mom raised her eyebrows.

"Hold it right there. Aren't you forgetting something?" she asked.

Kevin thought for a moment. Then he remembered. "Oh, that's right," he said, "I'm supposed to help Dad clean the garage today." Kevin looked unhappy. He mumbled to himself, "This is probably the only day I'll be able to fish, and now I'm stuck cleaning the garage."

"Ready, Kevin?" Dad asked, as he came into the kitchen.

"I guess so," said Kevin, following his Dad into the garage.

"Have fun," Mom called as the door closed behind them.

"Well, here's the plan," Dad stated as a big grin spread across his face. "I figure it'll take us an hour or so to get this place cleaned up. How about going fishing when we're done here?"

Kevin smiled. "This is going to be a good day after all," he said.

Read the above paragraph again. Then answer the questions.

4. What is Kevin's attitude about cleaning the garage? How can you tell?

_____

_____

_____

_____

5. What is Dad's attitude about the chore? How can you tell?

_____

_____

_____

_____

WRITER'S CRAFT

Comprehension and Language Arts Skills   **UNIT 4 • Lesson 5**   **127**

UNIT 4 Beyond the Notes • **Lesson 6** *Beethoven Lives Upstairs*

Commas

Commas have many functions in writing.

Rule	**Example**
▶ Use a comma after the greeting and closing of a friendly letter.	▶ Dear Cara, Your friend,
▶ Use a comma to set off direct quotes but not indirect statements.	▶ **"This young man will make a great name for himself in this world,"** Mozart supposedly said of Beethoven. (direct) My father said he enjoys the music of Beethoven. (indirect)
▶ Use a comma after a person's name or title in direct address.	▶ **Gina,** in what year was Beethoven born?
▶ Use a comma after introductory phrases and clauses.	▶ **On December 17, 1770,** Beethoven was baptized. (phrase) **When Haydn saw Beethoven's music,** he was impressed. (clause)
▶ Use a comma after a mild interjection.	▶ **Oh,** this music is so inspiring.
▶ Use commas before and after an interrupter.	▶ Beethoven, **as you may know,** lost his sense of hearing.
▶ Use a comma to separate items in a series.	▶ Beethoven composed nearly thirty-two sonatas, **including Sonata in C Sharp Minor, Moonlight Sonata, and Sonata in F Minor.**

 **Add commas where they are needed in the following sentences.**

1. For the next five years Beethoven remained in Bonn, Germany.

2. Before Beethoven left his hometown he was already considered a piano expert.

3. He is of course one of the best-known musicians who ever lived.

4. Boy I wish I could play like that.

5. Mozart Haydn Beethoven and Bach are among my favorite composers.

6. "Mom" Trevor asked "do you like Beethoven's music?"

UNIT 4 Beyond the Notes • **Lesson 6** *Beethoven Lives Upstairs*

▶ **Commas**

MECHANICS

Practice

Cross out commas where they are used incorrectly in the following sentences.

7. After he realized, he was going deaf, Beethoven's music changed.

8. His friends talked to him, through notes, when he totally lost his hearing.

9. It was not until 1819, that he lost his hearing.

10. It would be difficult, I would think, to write music, and not hear it.

11. Dan said, his father admires Beethoven for not quitting.

12. While walking, he drew many of his musical ideas in a sketchbook.

13. Today, those sketchbooks, show how he wrote his music.

14. He often worked on, more than one composition at a time.

Proofread

Correct the following letter by crossing out unnecessary commas and adding commas where needed.

Dear Lee

   Remember, when you asked me, if I would go to the symphony with you next week? Well Lee I think I'm going to change my mind. "You should just try something new" you told me. Well you are right. I heard some music by Beethoven today and was really impressed. If it's not too late will your parents still give me their extra ticket? Oh I'd really like to hear his music live. I want to hear, *Triple Concerto in C Major Wellington's Victory* and *Symphony Number Two in D Major.* Write back as soon as you can and let me know!

                                                   Your friend
                                                   Tony

Effective Beginnings and Endings

A good beginning catches the readers' attention, sets the tone of the writing, and reveals the topic of your writing.

▶ In the beginning of your story, tell about a problem.

▶ Use details that appeal to the senses.

▶ Ask questions.

▶ Use quotations or dialogue.

It is also important to have an effective ending to your story. One good way to end your story is by summarizing the main events. You can also restate the focus or the primary message of your story.

Try It! **The following opening paragraph could be made stronger. Revise the paragraph below using details, questions, and quotations to catch the readers' attention.**

Basketball is Dan's favorite sport. He plays every day if he can. All of his heroes are basketball players. His dream is to be like them.

_____

_____

_____

_____

_____

_____

_____

_____

_____

▶ Effective Beginnings and Endings

Practice

Revise the weak concluding paragraph below.

Dan's story proves that everyone should play basketball. Basketball is
the greatest sport ever invented.

_____

_____

_____

_____

_____

_____

_____

**Reread the beginning and concluding paragraphs you wrote
above. Tell what makes the revised paragraphs better than the
original ones.**

_____

_____

_____

_____

WRITER'S CRAFT

Sequence

Focus Good readers understand the sequence of events in a story in order to better comprehend what they are reading.

▶ The sequence of events is the order in which things happen in a story.
▶ Some time-and-order words that writers use to help readers understand the sequence of events in a story include *yesterday, tomorrow, this morning, first, last, after, next, finally,* and *then.*

Identify

Read the following sentences from the selection, and underline the time-and-order words.

1. In 1711, *Rinaldo*, Handel's first opera in Italian for English audiences, played for a remarkable 15 nights to packed houses at the new Haymarket Theatre.

2. At performances of *Amadigi* in 1715, the public kept clamoring to hear arias repeated until finally the theater management banned repetitions so that it could end before dawn.

3. Then, he picked her up and headed for the nearest sill.

4. There he sat each day in the bubbling water.

5. Several hours later, he had not returned for his next treatment.

6. He began the *Messiah* on August 22, and 23 days later he was done.

7. The next morning the wind had changed!

8. It was a hot, noisy crowd that Handel saw as he sat down at the harpsichord on April 13, 1742.

UNIT 4 Beyond the Notes • **Lesson 7** *The Man Who Wrote Messiah*

►**Sequence**

COMPREHENSION

Practice

Write five sentences, using time-and-order words, that show a sequence of events.

1. _____
   _____

2. _____
   _____

3. _____
   _____

4. _____
   _____

5. _____
   _____

Apply

Write a paragraph about an important goal you achieved through hard work and perseverance. Describe the steps or the process you used to obtain your goal. Use time-and-order words to make the sequence of events clear.

_____
_____
_____
_____
_____
_____
_____
_____
_____

UNIT 4 **Beyond the Notes • Lesson 7** *The Man Who Wrote* Messiah

Review

Parentheses, Hyphens, Dashes, Colons, and Commas

Add parentheses, hyphens, dashes, colons, and commas where they are needed.

1. "Sarah did you know" asked my sister "that more presidents came from Ohio than from any other state?"

2. "Well can you name them all?" asked my sister she's very persistent a minute later.

3. "No I can't name them all, but I do remember that Ulysses S. Grant Rutherford B. Hayes William McKinley and Warren G. Harding were all from Ohio" I answered.

4. William Tecumseh Sherman 1820–1891 was a famous Ohioan.

5. Ulysses S. Grant commander of the Union forces during the Civil War was also born in Ohio.

6. Although some people wanted President Lincoln to replace General Grant Lincoln defended Grant with these words "I can't spare him; he fights."

7. Other famous people born in Ohio include the following Annie Oakley Neil Armstrong and James Thurber.

8. Ohioan John Glenn became the first American to orbit Earth but not the first person in space in 1962.

9. An astronaut Yuri Gagarin from the Soviet Union now called the Russian Federation had been the first person in space the previous year.

10. John Glenn became the world's oldest space traveler he was seventy-seven years old when he joined the crew of the space shuttle *Discovery* in 1998.

11. During the nine day mission Glenn had many age related experiments performed on him.

12. In 1957 John Glenn an airplane pilot at that time made a record-breaking flight from Los Angeles to New York City.

▶ **Review**

▶ Indefinite, Interrogative, and Relative Pronouns

Circle the correct pronoun for each sentence and write whether it is indefinite, interrogative, or relative.

13. (Everyone/Anyone) knows that the Wright brothers made the first

successful airplane flight. _____

14. The brothers, (that/who) moved to Dayton, Ohio, owned a bicycle-

repair shop. _____

15. (Both/Either) had been interested in making flying machines for

many years before they designed their first successful airplane.

_____

16. (Who/Which) was the older brother, Orville or Wilbur Wright?

_____

17. The plane (that/which) the brothers first flew at Kitty Hawk is on

display at the Smithsonian Institution. _____

▶ Fragments

Write whether each item is missing a subject, a predicate, or both. If there is nothing missing, write *sentence* on the line.

18. This led to many successful flights. _____

19. Designed by the Wright brothers, the Wright flyer of 1903, the first

motor-powered airplane. _____

20. In 1892, the brothers opened a bicycle shop. _____

21. Which helped pay for their experiments. _____

22. Their first glider, which was tested in 1900. _____

23. Tested wing designs in wind tunnels. _____

24. For which they worked so hard. _____

GRAMMAR, USAGE, AND MECHANICS

Name _____   Date _____

Time and Order Words

You can use indicators of time and order to help your readers follow the sequence of events in your writing.

▶ Indicators of time are words that tell when events occur. Examples are *yesterday, tomorrow, this evening,* and *in 1799.*

▶ Indicators of order are words that show the sequence of events. Examples are *before, first, then,* and *at last.*

Underline the time and order words in the following sentences.

1. My sister graduated from high school in 1997.

2. Before you start to make dinner, please empty the dishwasher.

3. At last, I found a restaurant that I like.

4. Tomorrow, I plan on finishing the novel I started last week.

Read the following passage. Fill in the blanks using words or phrases that signal the sequence of events.

5. _____, my Aunt Maria took me to the music store so that I could pick out my birthday present—a new guitar!

6. _____ I could make my choice, however, I had to

consider several things. _____ I had to consider whether an acoustic or an electric guitar would be best for the kind of music I want to play.

7. _____ I had to consider whether the guitar would work

with the group I want to join. _____ I had to consider the cost.

8. _____ an hour, I finally made my choice.

UNIT 4 Beyond the Notes • **Lesson 7** *The Man Who Wrote Messiah*

▶ **Time and Order Words**

Practice

Read the paragraph. Then rewrite it using time and order words to help the reader understand when the events occured.

My parents, my sister, and I left the house. We arrived at the amusement park. My sister complained that she was hungry. We had some pastries at the French restaurant. I asked if we could ride the Monster Coaster. My mom said "yes." She and I headed toward the safari section of the park and got in line for the coaster. We waited. It started to rain. We left. We met up with my dad and my sister at the Enchanted Voyage ride. It was still raining. We each got passes to come back the next day.

_____

_____

_____

_____

_____

_____

_____

_____

_____

_____

_____

_____

WRITER'S CRAFT

UNIT 5 Ecology • **Lesson I** *Protecting Wildlife*

Fact and Opinion

Focus Good writers provide both facts and opinions in their writing to convey information.

> ▶ A **fact** is something that can be proven. Often, examples and statistics are used to support a fact.
>
> ▶ An **opinion** cannot be proven. It is a statement based on a person's beliefs. Facts, reasons, and examples may be used to support opinions.

Identify

Look through "Protecting Wildlife." Record two examples of facts and two examples of opinions presented by the author. Explain how the opinions are supported in the text.

Page _____ Fact: _____

_____

Page _____ Fact: _____

_____

Page _____ Opinion: _____

_____

How the opinion is supported: _____

_____

Page _____ Opinion: _____

_____

How the opinion is supported: _____

_____

UNIT 5 Ecology • **Lesson I** *Protecting Wildlife*

▶ Fact and Opinion

Practice

Read the following paragraph. What opinion does
the author express? Explain how the opinion is supported.

   Our national parks are in danger. Recent brush fires that swept through
Yosemite National Park and other western areas caused the destruction
of many acres of trees. The federal government has cut financial support
for the parks. Without financial support, the parks cannot be maintained
properly. Another danger to the parks is overcrowding. Each park
attracts thousands of tourists each year. National parks are our heritage.
We can't afford to ignore them.

1. Opinion: _____

   _____

   _____

2. How the opinion is supported: _____

   _____

   _____

3. Do you agree with the author's opinion? Why or why not?

   _____

   _____

Apply

Choose a subject and write a fact and an opinion about it. Explain how
the opinion differs from the fact.

_____

_____

_____

_____

_____

_____

COMPREHENSION

Name _____ Date _____

Subject-Verb Agreement

The subject of a sentence must agree in number with the verb.

Rule	**Example**
▶ A singular subject requires a singular verb.	▶ A **bat hunts** for food at night.
▶ A plural subject requires a plural verb.	▶ **Bats are** the only mammals that can fly.
▶ It may be difficult to find the subject of a sentence when a prepositional phrase separates the subject and the verb, but the same rules apply.	▶ Many **stories** about the vampire bat **are** not true.
▶ In an inverted sentence, the verb comes before the subject. To find the subject, rearrange the sentence so the subject comes first.	▶ Out of the cave **flew** the hungry **bat.** (inverted) The hungry **bat flew** out of the cave.

Underline the complete subject once. Underline its verb twice.

1. Many people fear bats.

2. Few people know much about bats.

3. Everyone thinks that bats like to get tangled in people's hair.

4. With great speed flies the bat.

5. Most bats, except for vampire bats, are harmless.

6. There are many kinds of bats.

7. Some species of bats grow to be about the size of a mouse.

8. One kind of bat has a wingspan of 3 feet.

9. Bats in most regions live in caves.

10. In the cave dwell hundreds of bats.

Comprehension and Language Arts Skills

UNIT 5 Ecology • **Lesson I** *Protecting Wildlife*

Subject-Verb Agreement

GRAMMAR AND USAGE

Practice

Circle the verb that correctly completes each sentence.

1. (Do/Does) the word *bats* send chills down your spine?

2. Everybody (is/are) going to the zoo tomorrow to see a bat.

3. Most students, probably in their science class, (are/is) going to study bats.

4. Bats, although they need much care, (make/makes) interesting pets.

5. The blood of mammals and large birds, (is/are) the food of choice for many bats.

6. Some other species, however, (feed/feeds) on the nectar or pollen of flowers.

7. Neither kind (pose/poses) a real threat to humans.

8. A bat, by consuming large amounts of insects, (help/helps) control the insect population.

9. There (are/is) bats in almost every country in the world.

10. Often, a colony of bats (infest/infests) a public building.

Proofread

Correct the errors in subject-verb agreement in the following paragraph.

The importance of bats are often greatly underestimated. Some kinds eats many insect pests. The Mexican free-tailed bats of Texas has been estimated to eat about 20,000 tons of insects per year. Other bats, which feed on plants, helps spread seeds so new plants will grow. Bats, contrary to popular belief, rarely attacks humans. These mammals, at least in parts of the East, is a symbol of good luck, long life, and happiness.

UNIT 5 Ecology • **Lesson I** *Protecting Wildlife*

Developing Persuasive Writing

Persuasive writing is used to convince readers to think, feel, or act a certain way. When writing to persuade, you will attempt to persuade readers to share your ideas about an issue.
▶ Support your viewpoint with facts and reasons.
▶ Appeal to the interests or emotions of the reader. Use words that are likely to affect or change the mind of the reader.

Read the following paragraph. What opinion does the author express? Explain how the opinion is supported.

Our national parks are in danger of extinction. Recent brushfires that swept through Yosemite National Park and other western areas caused the destruction of many acres of trees. Financial support for the parks from the federal government has dropped. Without financial support, the parks cannot be maintained properly. Another danger to the parks is overcrowding. Each park attracts thousands of tourists each year. National parks are our heritage. We can't afford to ignore them.

Opinion expressed by the author: _____

_____

How opinion is supported: _____

_____

Facts used to support opinion: _____

_____

_____

Other opinions used to support opinion: _____

_____

_____

UNIT 5 Ecology • **Lesson 1** *Protecting Wildlife*

Practice

Write a persuasive paragraph opposing the following topic.

Your school principal wants to put vending machines in the cafeteria.

_____

_____

_____

_____

_____

Write a persuasive paragraph supporting the topic.

_____

_____

_____

_____

_____

_____

UNIT 5 Ecology • **Lesson 2** *The Most Beautiful Roof in the World*

Direct and Indirect Objects

A direct object receives the action of a verb. An indirect object indirectly receives the action of a verb.

Rule

▶ A direct object answers the question *whom?* or *what?* after an action verb.

▶ An indirect object answers the question *to whom?* or *for whom?* an action is done. An indirect object always comes between the verb and the direct object.

▶ Both a direct and an indirect object may be compound.

▶ A transitive verb has a direct object, and an intransitive verb does not.

Example

▶ A zoologist studies **animals.**
I saw the **zoologist** observing a robin.

▶ Some birds feed their **chicks** worms.

▶ The robin eats **worms** and **berries.** (direct objects)
My grandparents feed **the robins** bird food. (indirect object)

▶ The bird **chirped** a warning from its nest. (transitive)
The bird **chirped** loudly. (intransitive)

Underline the direct object or objects in each sentence.

1. The robin pulled a worm out of the ground.

2. Robins feed their chicks worms and insects.

3. The female robin usually lays eggs in the spring.

4. Robins build their nests from grass and twigs.

5. Then, they plaster the insides of the nests with mud.

6. Sometimes robins use moss to line their nests.

7. The Indian robin has black plumage and a white shoulder patch.

8. Most robins inhabit forests, towns, and cities.

UNIT 5 Ecology • **Lesson 2** *The Most Beautiful Roof in the World*

Direct and Indirect Objects

Practice

Underline the direct object in each sentence once. If the sentence has an indirect object, circle it.

1. The zookeeper unlocked the gate.

2. She filled a bucket with fish for the dolphins.

3. The dolphins performed tricks for the zookeeper.

4. They even gave her kisses.

5. The zookeeper rewarded the dolphins.

6. She fed them fish.

7. She gave the dolphins a ball.

8. The dolphins made sounds in response.

9. The zookeeper showed the dolphins a new trick.

10. They performed the trick perfectly on their first try.

Proofread

Rewrite each sentence to change the prepositional phrase to an indirect object.

1. Many people give money to the zoo.

    _____

2. Zoo supporters often buy tickets for their friends.

    _____

3. The zoo's director gives interviews to reporters.

    _____

4. He offers discounts to students.

    _____

5. He also gives free parking to school buses.

    _____

GRAMMAR AND USAGE

UNIT 5 Ecology • **Lesson 2** *The Most Beautiful Roof in the World*

Staying on Topic

Whether you are writing to explain, inform, describe, or persuade, organize your ideas in paragraphs that stick to the topic.

Your readers expect to keep learning something new about your topic in each paragraph. Don't confuse them by putting in sentences that are not related to your topic.

▶ Make sure you have a topic sentence in each paragraph.

▶ All the other sentences in the paragraph will support your topic sentence.

▶ In each paragraph, delete, move, or revise any sentences that do not relate to your topic sentence.

Read the following paragraphs. Identify the topic of the paragraph, and write a strong topic sentence that expresses the main idea.

Presidential campaigns include posters, TV commercials, bumper stickers, and press conferences. The campaigns start years before the election and often cost millions of dollars. The campaign requires a staff of people to run it. The candidates hire campaign managers to take care of the business side of the campaign, which leaves them free to make speeches.

1. What is the topic of the paragraph?

_____

2. Write a strong topic sentence for the paragraph.

_____

_____

UNIT 5 Ecology • **Lesson 2** *The Most Beautiful Roof in the World*

Read the paragraph. Answer the questions.

In baseball, people don't try to hurt each other the way they do in football. I've played baseball, so I enjoy watching people who are really good at the game. I've never played football, so I don't appreciate professional players as much. I also like the atmosphere of baseball parks. They're much more parklike than football stadiums.

3. What is the topic of the paragraph?

_____

4. Write a strong topic sentence for the paragraph.

_____

Practice

Write a paragraph describing a career you are interested in trying. Underline your topic sentences, and make sure each sentence in your paragraph relates to the topic sentence.

_____

_____

_____

_____

_____

_____

_____

_____

_____

_____

WRITER'S CRAFT

UNIT 5 Ecology • **Lesson 3** *Alejandro's Gift*

Sequence

Focus Good writers arrange story events into a logical sequence so that readers can understand the order in which the events occur.

> **Time and order words** are important in explaining a sequence.
> ▶ Some words that indicate **time** are *yesterday, tomorrow, morning, night, moment, minute, suddenly,* and *last year.*
> ▶ Some words that indicate **order** are *first, last, after, next, finally,* and *then.*

Identify

Choose two sentences from "Alejandro's Gift" in which the author uses time and order words. Write down the time and order words and explain how they make the passage of time clear.

Page _____

Time and order words: _____

_____

How these words make the story clear: _____

_____

_____

Page _____

Time and order words: _____

_____

How these words make the story clear: _____

_____

_____

UNIT 5 Ecology • **Lesson 3** *Alejandro's Gift*

Practice

Rewrite the following list of steps as a paragraph that describes how to do laundry. Underline the time and order words you use.

1. Separate the dark-colored clothing from the light-colored clothing.

2. Check the pockets for tissues or change.

3. Put stain remover on any food or grass stains you find.

4. Begin running the water in the washing machine—warm water for whites and light colors, cold for dark colors.

5. Dissolve a cupful of detergent in the running water.

6. Place the clothes in the machine. Do not pack down. Close the lid.

_____

_____

_____

_____

_____

_____

_____

Apply

Write a paragraph about a meaningful event from your life. Use time and order words to make the sequence of events clear.

_____

_____

_____

_____

_____

_____

UNIT 5 Ecology • **Lesson 3** *Alejandro's Gift*

Perfect Tenses of Verbs

The present, past, and future perfect tenses of verbs tell when actions happen, happened, or will happen in relation to other actions or events.

Rule

▶ The present perfect tense of a verb expresses action that happened at an indefinite time in the past. Add *has* or *have* to the past participle of the verb to form the present perfect tense.

▶ The past perfect tense of a verb expresses action that happened before another action or event in the past. Add *had* to the past participle of the verb to form the past perfect tense.

▶ The future perfect tense expresses action that will be completed before another action or event begins. Add *will have* to the past participle of the verb to form the future perfect tense.

Example

▶ The meteorologist **has predicted** a storm.

▶ It **had begun** raining before we got to the car.

▶ The rain **will have stopped** by the time we are ready to go home.

Write *present perfect*, *past perfect*, or *future perfect* after each sentence to identify the tense of the underlined verb phrase.

1. It <u>has rained</u> all week. _____

2. One thunderstorm <u>had just passed</u> when clouds began to form

   again. _____

3. The rain <u>has flooded</u> the streets. _____

4. The storm <u>will have stopped</u> by tomorrow morning. _____

5. I <u>have lived</u> here all my life, but I've never seen so much rain. _____

GRAMMAR AND USAGE

▶ **Perfect Tenses of Verbs**

Practice

Rewrite each sentence, using the form of the verb shown.

Present Perfect

1. The hurricane (reach) the coast.

   _____

Past Perfect

2. The warning signal (blast) by the time we took shelter.

   _____

   _____

Future Perfect

3. We (experience) three hurricanes this year when this one is over.

   _____

   _____

Proofread

Replace the verbs that are used incorrectly with the present perfect, past perfect, or future perfect tense.

An avalanche will have crashed down the mountain. A layer of snow become unstable just before a group of skiers arrived. The group has just completed a run down the slope when the snow began to tumble down the mountain. Fortunately, the skiers will have gotten out of the way before the avalanche reached them. My family had vacationed here four years in a row when we go next year. I never had seen an avalanche so close.

UNIT 5 Ecology • **Lesson 3** *Alejandro's Gift*

Parallel Sentences

Rule	Example
▶ Make your sentences parallel. Words, phrases, or whole clauses joined by coordinating conjunctions, items linked in a series, items brought together by correlative conjunctions, and sentence elements (subject-verb-direct object) that are repeated within a sentence should all be parallel.	▶ Incorrect: The puppy likes to eat, sleep, and playing. Correct: The puppy likes to eat, to sleep, and to play. ▶ Incorrect: I placed my purse on the table and also my hat. Correct: I placed my purse and hat on the table.

Underline the parallel elements in each sentence.

1. Josh is not an outstanding diver or an outstanding swimmer.

2. I like reading, writing, and sewing.

3. Not only does she like pasta but she also likes fish.

4. He wrote that he likes London but that he does not like the weather.

5. Lou couldn't remember whether his mother asked him to buy cheddar cheese, swiss cheese, or mozzarella cheese.

 **UNIT 5** Ecology • **Lesson 3** *Alejandro's Gift*

▶ Parallel Sentences

Practice

Rewrite the following sentences, and make the elements of the sentences parallel.

6. Not only is Susan's son intelligent, but also creative.

_____

_____

7. Joy is, and has been, playing the piano for a long time.

_____

_____

8. My mother is taking me to the mall to buy new pants, sweaters, and new shoes.

_____

_____

9. Linda was not a boring person, and neither are her stories.

_____

_____

10. Joe forgot his camera, his coat, and map.

_____

_____

WRITER'S CRAFT

UNIT 5 Ecology • **Lesson 4** *A Natural Force*

Pronouns and Antecedents

A pronoun takes the place of a noun. An antecedent, which means "going before," is the noun to which a pronoun refers.

Rule

▶ The antecedent of a pronoun must be clear.

Example

▶ Yasushi prepared egg-drop soup for his father. He likes egg-drop soup. (unclear antecedent)
Yasushi prepared egg-drop soup for his father. His father likes egg-drop soup. (clear antecedent)
Yasushi prepared egg-drop soup for his father, who likes egg-drop soup. (clear antecedent)

 **Try It!** **Circle the antecedent of each underlined pronoun.**

1. Chinese cooks often stir-fry their food. First, <u>they</u> cut the food into bite-sized pieces.

2. A wok is used for stir-frying. <u>It</u> must be very hot before the food is added.

3. The chef cooked the meat first. Then, <u>he</u> added the vegetables.

4. The vegetables are added last because <u>they</u> cook more quickly than meat.

5. While the food is cooking, ginger and garlic are sometimes added to <u>it</u>.

6. If anyone wants the recipe for chicken stir fry, the chef will give it to <u>him or her</u>.

7. He also made noodle soup for my friends, and <u>they</u> loved <u>it</u>.

Pronouns and Antecedents

Practice

**Write the pronoun that correctly completes each sentence.
Underline the antecedent of each pronoun.**

1. Pearl S. Buck was an American writer who wrote many stories

   about life in China. _____ lived in China for many years.

2. Buck's parents were missionaries. They took _____ to China
   when she was very young.

3. Pearl S. Buck's books are still read throughout the world. _____
   have been translated into many languages.

Proofread

**Rewrite one or both sentences in each pair so that the antecedent
of each pronoun is clear.**

1. Wang Lung's wife, O-Lan, is a character in Pearl S. Buck's novel "The Good Earth."
   She had been a slave before she got married.

   _____

   _____

2. Wang Lung and O-Lan gradually bought small plots of land from
   various landowners. They endured many years of hardship.

   _____

   _____

3. When Wang Lung's first son was born, he was very happy.

   _____

   _____

4. Wang Lung had three sons, who also had children. They did not respect
   the land as their father had.

   _____

   _____

GRAMAMR AND USAGE

UNIT 5 Ecology • **Lesson 4** *A Natural Force*

Exaggeration

Rule	**Example**
▶ Exaggeration, which is also called hyperbole, is used for effect and is not to be taken literally. An exaggeration is an overstatement or a stretching of the truth to emphasize a point.	▶ She told him a million times to put the trash out on Tuesday.

Try It! **Read each sentence, and identify the over-statement or exaggeration used in each one.**

1. I am so tired that I think I could sleep for two weeks.

   _____

2. This book will bore you to death.

   _____

3. It's three o'clock, and I haven't eaten lunch. I am starving.

   _____

4. This chocolate cake is going to make me gain ten pounds.

   _____

5. My head aches, and it feels as if it is going to fall off.

   _____

6. That terrible music is killing me.

   _____

7. My dad is stronger than a horse.

   _____

UNIT 5 Ecology • **Lesson 4** *A Natural Force*

▶ Exaggeration

Practice

Write your own sentences using exaggeration.

8. _____

_____

9. _____

_____

10. _____

_____

11. _____

_____

12. _____

_____

Pick a story you have written and add exaggerations to create a vivid picture in your readers' minds. Rewrite the passage or paragraph below.

_____

_____

_____

_____

_____

_____

_____

_____

_____

_____

WRITER'S CRAFT

Cause and Effect

Focus Understanding what caused a character to behave in a certain manner or why an event occurred can contribute to a reader's involvement in a story.

▶ A cause is why something happens, and an effect are the things that happen.
▶ Writers often use signal words and phrases to identify cause-and-effect relationships. These words are called causal indicators and include *because, as, if, therefore, since, as a result*, and *for this reason*.

Identify

Look through "Saving the Peregrine Falcon," and identify cause-and-effect relationships. Complete the chart below.

Cause	Effect

Practice

Write the cause or effect of each example below.

1. Cause: Small birds that peregrines eat ingest grains and insects that have been sprayed with DDT.

   Effect: _____

2. Cause: Falcons have pointed wings.

   Effect: _____

3. Effect: Peregrine falcons used to be called duck hawks.

   Cause: _____

UNIT 5 Ecology • **Lesson 5** *Saving the Peregrine Falcon*

▶ **Cause and Effect**

Practice

Read the following paragraphs from the story, and write a sentence that shows the cause-and-effect relationship in each passage.

1. The peregrine's body, like those of other predatory birds, is well adapted for hunting. Its strong feet and sharp talons are ideal for catching and carrying, and its beak is designed for tearing. The peregrine's eyesight is so keen that it has been compared to a person being able to read a newspaper a mile away! A soaring peregrine can see a bird hundreds of feet below.

_____

_____

_____

_____

2. Scientists in the United States have found that DDT causes birds to lay eggs with shells that are too thin. When they measure the shells of hatched or broken eggs, they find that the thinnest shells are those with the most DDT in them. When parent birds sit on these eggs to keep them warm, the thin shells often break. Thin-shelled eggs also lose moisture faster than thick-shelled eggs. Often the chick growing inside the egg dies because the egg dries out too much. By helping the eggs with thin shells hatch, scientists can combat some of the effects of DDT.

_____

_____

_____

_____

3. It was important to keep the parent birds interested in the nest. After the eggs had hatched, the mountain climber would bring the babies back so that the parents could take care of them.

_____

_____

_____

_____

COMPREHENSION

Sentence Problems

Take a look at the following common sentence problems.

Rule	**Example**

▶ A run-on sentence is two or more sentences written as one sentence. Correct a run-on by writing separate sentences or by combining the sentences.

▶ Take out any redundant words or phrases in a sentence.

▶ A modifier (a descriptive word or phrase) should be placed as closely as possible to the word it modifies. If it is not, it is misplaced.

▶ There are large herds of caribou and they wander free in the arctic. (run-on)
There are large herds of caribou, **and** they wander free in the arctic. (correct)

▶ Always moving from place to place, caribou are migrating animals that wander and move south in the winter. (redundant)

▶ Caribou are migrating animals that move south in the winter. (correct)
Well adapted to their environment, the hooves of caribou help support them. (misplaced modifier)
Well adapted to their environment, **caribou have hooves** that help support them.

Write *run-on sentence, redundant words,* or *misplaced modifier* to identify the problem with each sentence.

1. Like many other animals, caribou also migrate as well.

_____

2. Migration is a yearly rhythm and it is the instinctual movement of animals and it requires strength and endurance.

_____

3. Ranging in length from 9 to 22 inches, the winter home of the arctic

tern is Antarctica. _____

4. Many other birds also migrate annually but none flies as far as the

arctic tern. _____

UNIT 5 Ecology • **Lesson 5** *Saving the Peregrine Falcon*

▶ **Sentence Problems**

Practice

Correct the sentences from Try It by rewriting them here.

1. _____

2. _____

   _____

   _____

3. _____

   _____

4. _____

   _____

Proofread

Rewrite the following passage so that all the sentences are correct.

Salmon migrate for long distances they travel from the ocean to the streams where they were born. Before mating, a nest is dug in the gravel by the female salmon. The adult salmon then float downstream and they return to the ocean, but when the young salmon hatch, they remain in the stream for about two years.

_____

_____

_____

_____

_____

_____

_____

GRAMMAR AND USAGE

UNIT 5 Ecology • **Lesson 5** *Saving the Peregrine Falcon*

Fact Versus Opinion

Writers often use facts and opinions in their writing. Facts can be proven true or false. Opinions are the writer's thoughts, beliefs, or feelings. They cannot be proven true or false. Facts help make writing more believable, and opinions help the reader understand the author's ideas. Writers often combine facts and opinions in the same piece of writing.

 **Identify the following statements as fact or opinion.**

1. Bats cannot see. Instead, they use their sense of hearing to guide them as they fly.

   _____

2. Jimmy's dog is the fastest one in the neighborhood.

   _____

3. Anacondas, which live in the rainforests of Brazil, can weight up to 200 pounds.

   _____

4. Some scientists believe an account that describes a 37-foot-long giant anaconda.

   _____

5. The candidate's political platform seems to be based on her interest in free school snacks.

   _____

6. The candidate for school president reported that, if elected, she will try to open the art room for recess activities.

   _____

Name _____ Date _____

▶ **Fact Versus Opinion**

Practice

Plan a magazine article about an actual event in your local
community. Decide on the event, then write three facts and three
opinions that you want to use in the article to make it believable.
You may want to refer to encyclopedias, newspapers, magazines,
or other sources.

Event: _____

Fact: _____

_____

Fact: _____

_____

Fact: _____

_____

Opinion: _____

_____

Opinion: _____

_____

Opinion: _____

_____

WRITER'S CRAFT

UNIT 5 Ecology • **Lesson 6** *The Day They Parachuted Cats on Borneo*

Review

Subject-Verb Agreement

Circle the verb that correctly completes each sentence.

1. Most types of jellyfish (live/lives) in all the oceans on Earth.

2. The bodies of most types (ranges/range) from 1 inch to more than 6 feet.

3. Out of the ocean depths (float/floats) a school of jellyfish.

4. Each one of the jellyfish (swim/swims) to the shore.

Direct and Indirect Objects

If the sentence has a direct object, underline it once. If the sentence has an indirect object, circle it.

1. Ecologists study living things in relation to their habitats.

2. Unfortunately, the animals in some ecosystems are endangered.

3. Ecologists sometimes give endangered animals a new chance for survival.

4. Some people write their congressional representatives letters.

5. Other supporters send conservation groups money.

Perfect Tenses of Verbs

Circle the correct tense of each verb.

1. Our ecology club (has raised/have raised) money to protect an endangered wetland ecosystem.

2. As soon as we (had finished/have finished) one fundraiser, we begin to plan another one.

3. By the end of this week, we (have raised/will have raised) more than five hundred dollars.

4. We (had considered/have considered) many ways to raise money before we decided on a car wash.

▶ **Pronouns and Antecedents**   ▶**Review**

Write the correct pronouns. Underline the antecedent of each one.

1. Mammals are warm-blooded animals that nurse their young.

   _____ are the only animals that have fur.

2. A female elephant usually has only one calf at a time. _____ might stay with its mother for more than ten years.

3. A mother deer teaches her fawn to stay close to her. _____ is always alert and protective of her fawn.

4. A beaver's teeth never stop growing; thus, _____ must eat

   continuously to keep _____ worn down.

▶ **Sentence Problems**

Rewrite the sentences so that they are correct.

1. Snapping turtles are aggressive they attack fish, lizards, and ducklings.

   _____

   _____

2. One of the most dangerous animals to humans is the crocodile, which is extremely dangerous and can hurt and even kill humans.

   _____

   _____

   _____

3. A fierce hunter that can move quickly through water, a turtle can rarely escape a crocodile.

   _____

   _____

   _____

UNIT 5 Ecology • **Lesson 6** *The Day They Parachuted Cats on Borneo*

Transition Words

Good writers use signal words and phrases, called transitions, to help readers understand the connection between ideas in a paragraph or passage. Transitions help readers understand the sequence of events in a story and where an action or event takes place.

▶ To show the **time,** use words such as *last week, today, tomorrow, at one o'clock, earlier,* and *yesterday.*

▶ To show the **order** of events, use words such as *first, next, finally,* and *last.*

▶ To show the **place or location,** use words such as *behind, nearby, to the right,* and *next to.*

▶ To **compare and contrast** two items, use words and phrases such as *in contrast, however, similarly,* and *also.*

▶ To **summarize** the main ideas, use words such as *in conclusion, therefore, to summarize,* and *as a result* to tie the main points together.

For each of the following paragraphs, identify all the transition words.

1. There is one thing that I find hard to believe about March 5, the day I broke my arm. First of all, I can't believe the technology doctors use to help heal their patients. Secondly, I had my arm examined by an x-ray. Then, I quickly had it set in a cast. After just a couple of hours, I was ready to leave the hospital.

2. When I decided to climb the mountain near my house, I became both elated and scared. I have never seen a mountain so large. Yesterday, I packed a backpack with supplies for the journey. I plan to start climbing when the sun rises and return home before dark.

3. Before child labor laws were passed, many children worked alongside the adults in factories all over the country. There were no safety precautions at the factories, so children often were hurt and even killed while doing their jobs. After child labor laws were passed, employers were forced to improve working conditions and could no longer hire children to work like adults.

Comprehension and Language Arts Skills

UNIT 5 Ecology • **Lesson 6** *The Day They Parachuted Cats on Borneo*

▶**Transition Words**

Practice

Use the information below to write a paragraph in which you make the description clear through the use of place and location words.

4. To attract more birds

5. We decided to build a birdhouse

6. The oak tree

7. The longest limb

8. We used a ladder

9. We looked at the birds

_____

_____

_____

_____

_____

_____

_____

_____

_____

_____

WRITER'S CRAFT

Author's Purpose

Focus The author's purpose is his or her reason for writing.

> ▶ Every author has a purpose for writing a story. The author's purpose may be to inform, to explain, to entertain, or to persuade.
>
> ▶ An author may have more than one purpose in writing.

Identify

Look through "King Midas" and identify the author's purposes for writing the fable. Find three examples that illustrate the author's purposes for writing.

Author's purposes for writing the fable: _____

_____

_____

Example: _____

_____

_____

Example: _____

_____

_____

Example: _____

_____

_____

Comprehension and Language Arts Skills

UNIT 6 A Question of Value • **Lesson I** *King Midas*

Practice

Read through other selections you have read in the **Anthology**, and identify the author's purpose for writing the selections. Find examples that illustrate the author's purpose for writing the story. Choose one nonfiction selection and one fiction selection.

Nonfiction selection: _____

Author's purpose for writing the story: _____

_____

Example: _____

_____

_____

Fiction selection: _____

Author's purpose for writing the story: _____

_____

Example: _____

_____

_____

Apply

Identify something that you value as much as the king valued gold. Write a short paragraph informing the reader why you value the object.

_____

_____

_____

_____

_____

_____

UNIT 6 A Question of Value • **Lesson I** *King Midas*

Review

Verbs

Underline each verb that expresses a state of being. Circle each action verb.

1. Canada is a huge country.

2. Few people live in northern Canada.

3. Snow and ice cover northern Canada for most of the year.

4. Herds of moose inhabit the northern forests.

5. The forests are also home to caribou, beavers, and muskrats.

6. Numerous bighorn sheep climb the steep Rocky Mountains.

7. The Arctic Ocean borders Canada's northwestern shore.

8. Some sections of Canada seem more French than British.

9. In 1763, Canada became a British colony by the terms of the Treaty of Paris.

10. In addition to the Great Lakes, Canada has more than forty large lakes.

Pronouns

Circle the correct pronouns.

11. (We/Us) Americans are on friendly terms with our northern neighbors, the Canadians.

12. My friend and (me/I) have studied the history of Canada in school.

13. (Their's/Theirs) is a great country, just as (ours/our's) is.

14. Canada received (its/it's) full independence from Great Britain in 1926.

15. During World War II, Canadian Prime Minister William King and U.S. President Franklin D. Roosevelt united (their/they're) countries with a defense agreement.

Comprehension and Language Arts Skills

UNIT 6 A Question of Value • **Lesson I** *King Midas*

► Subjects and Predicates

Underline the simple subject once and the simple predicate twice.

16. The first person from Europe to reach Canada was John Cabot, a navigator from Italy.

17. King Henry VII of England sent Cabot on his voyage.

18. In 1497, John Cabot sailed across the Atlantic Ocean.

19. He revisited the northeastern coast of North America the following year.

20. In 1534, Jacques Cartier, an explorer from France, landed on the Bell Isle Strait.

► Proper Nouns and Capitalization

Draw three lines under any letters that should be capitalized. Draw a slash through each capitalized letter that should be lowercase.

21. The Strait led to a large bay between two islands that are now called newfoundland and labrador.

22. The Bay soon became known as the gulf of St. Lawrence.

23. The long River that runs between the Bay and Lake Ontario was named the St. Lawrence river.

24. Another French Explorer, champlain, discovered the ottowa river in 1613; he also discovered lake huron and lake ontario in 1615.

25. The iroquois, huron, and algonquin people were natives of the Region around St. Lawrence, which was called new france by the French settlers.

UNIT 6 A Question of Value • **Lesson 1** *King Midas*

Sensory Detail

Rule	**Example**
▶ Sensory details are words or phrases that appeal to the senses. They describe how something looks, smells, tastes, sounds, or feels. Writers often use sensory details to describe what characters in the story hear, smell, taste, touch, and see. This helps readers picture or feel what is happening in the story.	▶ Melissa opened the door, and the icy wind gripped her. The snow crunched under her feet as she walked quickly to the car. Her fingers stung from the bitter cold. Even her thickest, warmest gloves couldn't resist the –20° temperatures.

Read the following passage. Write the sensory details on the appropriate line.

Zeke spied the shiny, new blue-and-white box of Frosty Treats on the shelf. He tore open the box top, and the sweet scent of honey and cinnamon wafted up to his nose. The crispy pieces of cereal were shaped like the letter "K"; Zeke popped one into his mouth—it tasted just like a cinnamon bun.

The cereal made a bright, tinkling noise as it hit the bowl. He grabbed the cold, wet container of milk, took off the lid, and a sour, buttery smell hit the air.

"Gross! This milk expired last week!" Zeke exclaimed. Deciding to eat the cereal anyway, he scooped a big spoonful into his mouth and crunched loudly.

Sight: _____

Smell: _____

Sound: _____

Taste: _____

Touch: _____

Sensory Detail

Practice

Look out a window and write a paragraph about what you see, using the best words you can think of to let your reader know what sense impressions you are receiving.

_____

_____

_____

_____

_____

_____

_____

Now close your eyes and think about what you hear and smell. Then write a paragraph using sensory descriptions to describe what you smell and hear.

_____

_____

_____

_____

_____

_____

_____

WRITER'S CRAFT

UNIT 6 A Question of Value • **Lesson 2** *A Brother's Promise*

Review

Kinds of Sentences

Add the correct end punctuation to each sentence and identify it as a declarative, interrogative, imperative, or exclamatory sentence.

1. Have you ever seen a live rattlesnake _____

2. I recently saw one in my back yard _____

3. It slithered along the grass and made a buzzing sound ____

   _____

4. I was so frightened I didn't know what to do ____

   _____

5. Don't let that stop you from seeing the snakes at the zoo ____

   _____

Adjectives and Adverbs

Underline the adjectives once and draw an arrow from each adjective to the word that it modifies. Circle the adverbs and draw an arrow from each adverb to the word that it modifies.

6. Rattlesnakes usually live in hot, dry areas.

7. They often rattle the hollow scales at the ends of their tails.

8. The rattling sound is actually a sharp warning for intruders not to come near the snake.

9. When a rattlesnake sinks its sharp, pointed fangs into its prey, poison quickly squeezes from the sacs to the fangs.

10. When the rattlesnake is not using its deadly fangs, they fold closely against the top of its mouth.

UNIT 6   A Question of Value • **Lesson 2** *A Brother's Promise*

GRAMMAR, USAGE, AND MECHANICS

▶ Prepositions

Circle the prepositional phrases. Underline each object of the preposition.

16. New Mexico is located in the southwestern part of the United States.

17. New Mexico is bordered by Colorado to the north, Oklahoma and Texas to the east and south, and Arizona to the west.

18. Mountains and deserts stretch across most of the state.

19. The Continental Divide runs along the western part of New Mexico, and the Rio Grande runs through the middle of the state.

20. As the Rio Grande flows out of New Mexico, it forms the border between Texas and New Mexico.

▶ Quotation Marks and Underlining

Add quotation marks or underlining where they are necessary.

26. What is your favorite book? asked Tracy.

27. It's hard to say which is my very favorite, I answered, but Charlotte's Web is one of my favorites.

28. The book Where the Sidewalk Ends includes the poem Hug O' War.

29. I enjoyed an article that recently appeared in National Geographic magazine called Polar Bears: First Cubs on the Ice.

30. The New York Times and The Wall Street Journal are daily newspapers.

▶ Linking Verbs, Predicate Nouns, and Predicate Adjectives

Circle the linking verbs. Underline the predicate nouns once and the predicate adjectives twice.

31. A lizard's skin feels tough and scaly.

32. The anole lizard's claws are sharp, which helps them climb trees quickly.

33. One relative of the anole is the gecko, a small, harmless lizard.

34. Lizards seem slow and lazy; however, most of them are quick.

UNIT 6 **A Question of Value • Lesson 2** *A Brother's Promise*

Organizing a Descriptive Paragraph

A descriptive paragraph includes sensory details that create a mental picture of an object, a person, a setting, an action, or an event.

Details in a descriptive paragraph need to be presented in a sensible order. Writers can order details in their descriptive paragraphs in several ways: top to bottom, near to far, left to right, or focal point. Ordering your details according to where they are in the picture you are creating for the reader is called spatial order.

Transition words and phrases, such as *over*, *beside*, and *in the corner*, help show how the details in a descriptive paragraph are related.

 **Read the following paragraph. Then answer the questions.**

    Jill rubbed her cool hands near the warm, crackling fire. She bit into the last gooey, toasted marshmallow and sat back to enjoy the moment. Surrounding her was the loud but soothing noise of chirping crickets. A slight breeze blew, rustling the leaves in the nearby trees. Tiny lights flashed in the woods as the fireflies floated in the dark. Jill's brothers laughed and played card games in their tent at the edge of the campground. Looking up at the night sky from her spot next to the fire, she could see the constellation Orion; the three stars that make up his belt sparkled brightly. Suddenly, a wolf howled in the distance.

1. How did the writer order the details in the paragraph—top to bottom, near to far, left to right, or focal point? Explain your answer.

    _____

    _____

2. Name three sensory details the writer used to describe the scene.

    _____

    _____

3. Name three transition words or phrases the writer used:

    _____

    _____

Name _____ Date _____

▶ **Organizing a Descriptive Paragraph**

Think of a scene you could describe in a descriptive paragraph. Draw a sketch of the scene below.

Sketch:

On the lines below, write some of the sensory details you would include in your descriptive paragraph. How would you order the details?

_____

_____

_____

_____

_____

WRITER'S CRAFT

Exact Words

> Exact words are exact in the way they describe people, things, or actions. They give the reader a clear picture and express exactly what the writer wants to say.
>
> **Rule**
>
> ▶ Replace general nouns and adjectives with more specific, descriptive words.
>
> ▶ Replace general verbs with more precise ones. You may also add adverbs to describe the action more vividly.
>
> **Example**
>
> ▶ My sandwich tasted awful. (general words)
> My tuna sandwich tasted dry and fishy. (exact words)
>
> ▶ I went to the chalkboard. (general verb)
> I practically dragged myself to the chalkboard. (exact words)

 **Try It!**   **Rewrite each sentence, changing the underlined word or words to make them more exact and vivid.**

1. My parents gave me <u>some clothes</u> for my birthday. _____

   _____

2. The beach was <u>beautiful</u>. _____

   _____

3. I <u>put</u> my report card on the refrigerator door. _____

   _____

4. "Leave me alone!" he <u>said</u> as he <u>closed</u> his bedroom door. _____

   _____

5. The <u>giant</u> <u>threw</u> the stone into the <u>river</u>. _____

   _____

UNIT 6 A Question of Value • **Lesson 2** *A Brother's Promise*

Practice

Rewrite the following paragraph, replacing the underlined words with more exact, vivid ones. In some cases, simply add adjectives or adverbs to the underlined word.

The door <u>opened</u>, and <u>my sister</u> <u>came</u> into the <u>room</u> carrying a <u>turtle</u>. "Look what I found <u>walking</u> across our sidewalk," she <u>said</u>. "Are you sure there's a turtle in there?" I <u>asked</u>. All I could see was a <u>shell</u>. My sister <u>laughed</u>. "Yes, it has a <u>head</u>, a <u>tail</u>, and <u>four legs</u>—I saw them myself." Just then, the shell <u>moved</u>, and I could see two <u>eyes</u> <u>looking</u> out at me. "We can't keep it," I <u>said</u>. "I know," she <u>said</u>, "but I thought it wouldn't mind a short vacation."

_____

_____

_____

_____

_____

_____

_____

_____

_____

_____

_____

_____

_____

_____

_____

_____

_____

Review

Helping Verbs and Double Negatives

Circle the words in parentheses that correctly complete the sentences. Underline the helping verb(s) in each sentence.

1. I haven't (ever/never) seen an owl up close, but I am really interested in owls.

2. Did you hear the owl hooting in the distance last night?

3. Many owls don't have (anywhere/nowhere) to nest and hunt safely because of forest development.

Clauses and Conjunctions

Underline the main clause in each of the following sentences. Add commas where they are needed.

4. Because of their secretive habits and weird calls owls have become objects of superstition.

5. Owls which are nocturnal animals, hunt mostly at night.

6. From grasslands to rain forests owls live in almost any habitat.

7. Some owls catch their prey by dropping from the edge of forest openings.

Reflexive and Intensive Pronouns

Circle the correct pronouns.

8. Mr. Perez asked Scott and (me/myself) to write reports about woodland animals.

9. We found (ourself/ourselves) getting really interested in the topic.

10. Some woodland animals feed (theirselves/themselves) well in the fall and then hibernate in a dry, sheltered den for the winter.

11. Sometimes, the bear (himself/itself) will dig the den.

▶ Participles and Participial Phrases   ▶Review

Underline the participles and participial phrases. Draw an arrow to the noun or pronoun that each participle or participial phrase modifies.

12. The owl, perched high atop the tree, searches the ground.

13. Swooping down from the tree, the owl lunges for a mouse.

14. The scampering mouse heads for a hollow log.

15. The owl's hunting skills prove superior.

16. Her chirping chicks wait for their food.

17. Satisfied with their meal, the chicks fall back asleep.

▶ Types of Sentences

Write whether each sentence is simple, compound, complex, or compound-complex.

18. Tawny owls live in woodlands; the owls' multicolored markings allow them to blend in with their environment.

   _____

19. Owls are successful predators, because they have keen eyesight and

   sharp hearing. _____

20. Owl's flight feathers are light and soft, and their silent flight allows them to hear the slightest noises made by their prey.

   _____

21. The eyes of an owl are very large. _____

GRAMMAR AND USAGE

UNIT 6 A Question of Value • **Lesson 3** *A Gift for a Gift*

The Sound of Language

In writing, the sounds of words are important. Make your writing more vivid and interesting by using the following techniques.

Rule

▶Alliteration is the repetition of consonant sounds at the beginning of words.

▶Onomatopoeia occurs when a word read aloud sounds like what it actually is.

▶End rhyme is the rhyming of words at the end of lines of poetry.

▶Internal rhyme is the rhyming of words within one line of writing.

▶Repetition is the repeating of words or phrases to give rhythm to your writing.

▶Rhythm is the pattern of accented and unaccented syllables in a line of poetry or prose.

 **Try It!** Read each of the following examples and identify the sound of language used in each.

1. The booming thunder and crashing lightning scared our dog.

   _____

2. I confess that my room is a mess.

   _____

3. Every time the boat rose and fell, rose and fell, my stomach rose and fell, rose and fell with it.

   _____

4. It was a dreary, dull, dismal day.

   _____

5. I hear that happy song again.

   _____

6. Little boys love tales
   Of snakes and snails.

   _____

▶ **The Sound of Language**

Practice

Write an example sentence using the following sounds of language.

Alliteration: _____

_____

Onomatopoeia: _____

_____

End Rhyme: _____

_____

Internal Rhyme: _____

_____

Repetition: _____

_____

Rhythm: _____

_____

WRITER'S CRAFT

UNIT 6 A Question of Value • **Lesson 4** *The Gold Coin*

Author's Purpose

Focus The author's purpose is his or her reason for writing.

> ▶ Every author has a purpose for writing a story. The author's purpose may be to inform, to explain, to entertain, or to persuade.
>
> ▶ An author may have more than one purpose in writing.

Identify

Look through "The Gold Coin" and identify examples of the author's purposes for writing the story. Find three examples that illustrate the author's purposes for writing.

Page: _____

Example: _____

_____

_____

Page: _____

Example: _____

_____

_____

Page: _____

Example: _____

_____

_____

Comprehension and Language Arts Skills

UNIT 6 A Question of Value • **Lesson 4** *The Gold Coin*

Practice

Find two stories you have read, one nonfiction and one fiction, and identify the author's purpose for writing the stories. Find examples that illustrate the author's purpose for writing the story.

Nonfiction selection: _____

Author's purpose for writing the story: _____

_____

_____

Example: _____

_____

_____

Fiction selection: _____

Author's purpose for writing the story: _____

_____

_____

Example: _____

_____

_____

Apply

Find a story you have written and identify the purpose you had for writing the story. Give examples that illustrate your purpose for writing the story.

Author's purpose for writing the story: _____

_____

Example of author's purpose: _____

_____

Example of author's purpose: _____

_____

COMPREHENSION

UNIT 6   A Question of Value • **Lesson 4** *The Gold Coin*

Review

Parentheses, Hyphens, Dashes, Colons, and Commas

Add parentheses, hyphens, dashes, colons, and commas where they are needed.

1. "Jackie have you ever heard of Wilma Rudolph?" asked my friend Kali.

2. "Yes I have" I answered. "She was a famous Olympic gold medalist runner."

3. Wilma Rudolph 1940–1994 overcame incredible difficulties to become a champion runner.

4. Wilma Rudolph's father a tobacco plant worker had twenty two children.

5. When Wilma Rudolph was four years old an illness I'm not sure what it was left her left leg paralyzed.

6. Wilma Rudolph slowly regained her ability to walk after receiving massages from her family members using a leg brace and then wearing orthopedic shoes shoes that help a person learn to walk.

7. When Rudolph was thirteen she was able to walk and run so she tried out for her high school basketball team.

8. Her coach Clinton Gray nicknamed the thirteen year old girl "Skeeter."

9. He explained to her why he called her "Skeeter" with these words "You're little you're fast and you always get in my way."

10. After a year of running track in high school Rudolph qualified for the 1956 U.S. Olympic team.

11. Before the 1960 Olympics Rudolph suffered the following setbacks a pulled thigh muscle complications from a tonsil operation and a case of the flu.

12. She won three gold medals for these events the one-hundred meter dash the two-hundred-meter dash and the relay.

13. Truly the story of Wilma Rudolph is amazing.

Comprehension and Language Arts Skills

▶ Pronouns

Choose the correct pronoun in each sentence.

14. Wilma Rudolph, (who/that) hadn't even been able to walk for several years during her childhood, had become the world's fastest woman.

15. (Anyone/No one) could have imagined that this would be possible.

16. (Both/Either) her determination and her joy in being able to run helped Wilma Rudolph overcome incredible difficulties.

17. (Who/Whom) else do you know that has such courage?

18. Not (much/many) of the people I know could have handled the same challenges with grace and strength.

19. Hers is a story (that/which) should be told for generations to come.

▶ Fragments

Join the following sentences to omit the fragments.

20. As she crossed the finish line for the team relay race. Wilma Rudolph secured her third gold medal.

21. Rudolph was not only fast. But also was a graceful runner with long strides.

22. Wilma Rudolph, called "The Gazelle" by fans at the 1960 Olympics. She was a favorite among spectators and journalists.

23. Fans loved her because of her gentle, kind manner. And her beautiful running style.

24. A truly great athlete and admirable person. Wilma Rudolph set up a charity to help underprivileged children and teenagers.

GRAMMAR, USAGE, AND MECHANICS

UNIT 6 A Question of Value • **Lesson 4** *The Gold Coin*

The Sound of Language

Writing that uses the sound of language captures the reader's attention. The techniques described below can give rhythm and vividness to your poetry or prose.

Rule
▶ Alliteration is the repetition of consonant sounds at the beginning of words.
▶ Onomatopoeia occurs when the sound of a word makes the reader think of its meaning.
▶ End rhyme is the rhyming of words at the end of lines of poetry.
▶ Internal rhyme is the rhyming of words within one line of writing.
▶ Repetition is the repeating of words or phrases to make an impact on the reader.

 **Try It!** **Identify the underlined techniques in the following sentences.**

1. The bee buzzed in my ear. _____

2. The wind whipped through the windows. _____

3. He could hear the bang, bang, bang of a shutter hitting the side

   of the house. _____

4. The rain came pounding down as I boarded the train. _____

5. It was a big, big mess. _____

6. I listened to the low lilting music as I lounged in the lobby. _____

7. Under the hot July sun
   On the beach we had so much fun. _____

8. Round and round the Ferris wheel spun. _____

UNIT 6 A Question of Value • **Lesson 4** *The Gold Coin*

▶ The Sound of Language

Practice

Write an imaginative story using various techniques to make the sound of your language interesting.

_____

_____

_____

_____

_____

_____

_____

_____

_____

_____

_____

_____

_____

_____

_____

_____

_____

_____

_____

WRITER'S CRAFT

UNIT 6   A Question of Value • **Lesson 5** *The No-Guitar Blues*

Review

Subject-Verb Agreement

Circle the verb that agrees with the subject in each sentence.

1. There (are/is) many players practicing on the field.

2. This roster of players' names (belong/belongs) to the coach.

3. Through the crowds of people (sails/sail) the soccer ball.

Direct and Indirect Objects

If the sentence has a direct object, underline it. If the sentence has an indirect object, circle it.

4. The soccer coach is conducting a practice.

5. The coach sends notes of encouragement.

6. She gives the players confidence in their abilities.

7. The players work well together.

8. The team gives our school pride.

Perfect Tenses of Verbs

Circle the correct tense of each verb and write whether it is present perfect, past perfect, or future perfect.

9. Our soccer team (has won/had won) five games so far this season.

    _____

10. By the end of the season, we (have improved/will have improved)

    our record since last year. _____

11. We (had practiced/have practiced) for many weeks before we

    began working well as a team. _____

12. After we (had played/will have played) our first game, we knew

    that we would have a good team. _____

UNIT 6 A Question of Value • **Lesson 5** *The No-Guitar Blues*

▶ **Pronoun-Antecedent Agreement**   ▶**Review**

**Write the correct pronouns on the lines. Draw an arrow from each
pronoun to its antecedent.**

13. Pelé was one of the greatest soccer players of all time.

    _____ was only seventeen years old when he played in

    _____ first World Cup game.

14. He led Brazil to _____ third World Cup championship
    in 1970.

15. The Brazilians are known as the most dedicated soccer fans in the

    world; _____ wept when Pelé announced his retirement.

▶ **Sentence Problems**

Rewrite the sentences so that they are correct.

16. Scoring ninety-seven international goals in his career, the world
    record is held by Pelé.

    _____

    _____

    _____

17. Pelé has scored 1,281 goals in his entire professional career and he
    also holds the world record for the most three-goal games.

    _____

    _____

    _____

18. Most soccer fans consider the soccer player Pelé to be the most
    talented soccer player in the world who ever lived in the world.

    _____

    _____

    _____

GRAMMAR AND USAGE

Figurative Language

A figure of speech is an expression in which words do not have their real meanings but are used to create pictures in the readers' mind. There are several kinds of figures of speech, also called figurative language.

Rule	**Example**
▶ A simile compares two different things by using the words *like* or *as*.	▶ The wood was as smooth as silk.
▶ A metaphor compares two different things without using the words *like* or *as*.	▶ The leaves were a blanket under which I snuggled.
▶ Personification gives human qualities to an object or idea.	▶ The music danced in my mind as I left the theater.

Try It! **Identify the type of figurative language used in each example.**

1. Time marched on, and soon it was August. _____

2. The dome on the top of the building looked like a child's knit cap. _____

3. A book is a ticket to adventure. _____

4. Her temper tantrums were as forceful as a tornado. _____

5. My computer thinks that it has all of the answers. _____

6. The tree's blossoms were tiny teacups catching the rain. _____

► **Figurative Language**

Practice

Look through stories you have read for examples of figures of speech. Write two examples of each figure of speech.

7. Simile: _____

_____

_____

8. Metaphor: _____

_____

_____

9. Personification: _____

_____

_____

Write your own sentences using different figures of speech.

10. Simile: _____

_____

_____

11. Metaphor: _____

_____

_____

12. Personification: _____

_____

_____

WRITER'S CRAFT

UNIT 6 A Question of Value • **Lesson 6** *The Quiltmaker's Gift*

Drawing Conclusions

Focus Good readers use information in the text to draw conclusions about characters and events in a story.

> ▶ Authors do not always provide complete and explicit descriptions of or information about characters and events in a story. Readers can use clues or suggestions provided by an author to draw conclusions about characters and events in a story.
>
> ▶ Conclusions are always supported by evidence from the text.

Identify

Look through "The Quiltmaker's Gift" for information that can be used to draw conclusions about the characters and events in the story. Write the conclusions drawn and the information from the text used to draw the conclusions.

1. Conclusion: _____

_____

Text evidence used to draw conclusion: _____

_____

2. Conclusion: _____

_____

Text evidence used to draw conclusion: _____

_____

3. Conclusion: _____

_____

Text evidence used to draw conclusion: _____

_____

Comprehension and Language Arts Skills

UNIT 6 A Question of Value • **Lesson 6** *The Quiltmaker's Gift*

Drawing Conclusions

Practice

Pick an interesting scene or event from another fable you have read, and rewrite it in your own words. Include any conclusions drawn about the characters or events in this scene.

_____

_____

_____

_____

_____

COMPREHENSION

Review

Parts of Speech

Identify each noun by circling it and writing *n* above it. Underline the verbs and prepositional phrases in the sentences below and write *v* or *p* above them.

1. The Great Lakes were formed at the end of the last ice age.

2. Five huge basins had been gouged from the land by glaciers.

3. Then, water from the melted ice of the glaciers filled the basins.

4. Michigan is surrounded by four of the Great Lakes.

5. The Great Lakes provide entertainment for Michigan residents and visitors.

Subjects and Predicates

Draw a vertical line between the complete subject and complete predicate in each sentence. Underline each simple subject once and each simple predicate twice.

6. Lake Erie, Lake Superior, Lake Huron, and Lake Michigan surround Michigan.

7. Michigan contains thousands of smaller lakes and also has many rivers.

8. The rivers flow through forests and spill over small cliffs.

9. The Upper Peninsula of Michigan is linked to the Lower Peninsula by a bridge.

10. Cliffs, arches, and caves have been carved by erosion into the rocks of Pictured Rocks National Lakeshore.